THE
BEGINNING OF
BETTER DAYS

THE
BEGINNING OF
BETTER DAYS

❦❀❦

Divine Instruction to Women
FROM THE PROPHET
Joseph Smith

WITH PERSONAL INSIGHTS FROM
Sheri Dew AND Virginia H. Pearce

DESERET
BOOK

SALT LAKE CITY, UTAH

Library of Congress Cataloging-in-Publication Data
Dew, Sheri L., author.
  The beginning of better days : divine instruction to women from the prophet Joseph Smith / Sheri Dew and Virginia H. Pearce.
     pages cm.
  Includes bibliographical references and index.
  ISBN 978-1-60641-851-2 (hardbound : alk. paper)
  1. Women—Religious aspects—The Church of Jesus Christ of Latter-day Saints.   2. Relief Society (The Church of Jesus Christ of Latter-day Saints)   3. Women—Conduct of life.   I. Pearce, Virginia H., author.   II. Title.
  BX8643.W66D49 2012
  248.8'430882893—dc23   2012003586

Printed in the United States of America
Lake Book Manufacturing, Inc., Melrose Park, IL

10   9   8   7   6   5   4   3   2   1

CONTENTS

❧❀☙

PREFACE

❦❀❧

The record kept by Eliza R. Snow of the proceedings of the Female Relief Society of Nauvoo has been referred to for years, but it was not readily accessible to all interested parties until its relatively recent inclusion in the Joseph Smith Papers project. Now photographs of the original pages appear online alongside their typed transcriptions in a document titled "Nauvoo Relief Society Minute Book" at josephsmithpapers.org.

Latter-day Saint women are incredibly fortunate that Eliza was foresighted enough to preserve the Minute Book and carry it across the plains with her, allowing access to the original, historically significant document exactly as it was created. And when that document was being prepared for inclusion in the Joseph Smith Papers, people who had long been associated with the Minutes suggested to the two of us that perhaps something should be done to bring them even more into the light. Specifically, buried within the Minutes are notes of six sermons that the Prophet Joseph delivered to the Relief Society between March and August 1842. This priceless record of instruction delivered by the Prophet of the Restoration directly and particularly to women has been quoted in bits and pieces, but too few people have studied his words in depth.

Each of us became acquainted with these teachings at different stages and for different reasons, but we both came to them with high motivation to try to come to grips with the kinds of questions that almost inevitably occur in the lives of faithful Latter-day Saint women. We wanted to know where women "fit" in the plan of salvation. What did the Lord expect of His daughters? What blessings did He have in store for us, and how could we lay hold upon those blessings? In Joseph Smith's teachings to the Relief Society, we each found a treasure of guidance, motivation, pure doctrine, and wise prophetic counsel.

So we were intrigued by the opportunity we saw to provide some context for these sermons and especially to help open them up to a wider readership. Our first task was to comb through the Minutes and attempt to extract the sermons themselves from the general business of the Relief Society. This we have done to the best of our ability, trying in most cases to include only the portions attributed to Joseph Smith— although in the case of the inaugural meeting (March 17, 1842) we have included the energetic discussion between the women and their priesthood leaders that led to the official name of the Relief Society. With a handful of exceptions (noted in brackets) we have retained original spelling and punctuation, presenting the words just as they appear in Eliza's record.

As it turned out, that proved to be the easy part. As we began to put our personal insights on paper, we were both, quite frankly, terrified. Our fear at being seen as embellishing and interpreting Joseph Smith's words caused each of us to stop, dead in our tracks, more than once. But then our excitement over the power of his words in our own lives would eventually drag us back again and again to this project. After all, the possibility of being misunderstood is an occupational hazard for anyone who attempts to arrange words on paper.

One challenge is that the six sermons delivered by the Prophet Joseph Smith do not read the way talks in our modern era do. As with most of the talks attributed to him, they were written down by someone in attendance—in this case, Eliza R. Snow. They come across very much as notes, lapsing in and out of the first-person voice, filled with shortcuts and abbreviations, with little attention to stylistic consistency. We can almost see Eliza writing as fast as she could, trying to keep up with the instruction coming from the Prophet, capturing as much as possible the key points and the spirit of his messages.

Reading these talks, then, is not like reading the conference issue of the *Ensign*. We encourage you to move slowly, considering individual statements, seeking confirmation of the Spirit for conclusions reached, studying, examining, treasuring. Space has been provided at the bottom of each page in the section containing Joseph Smith's teachings so that you can make your own notes. In the introductory essays, we have attempted to share a little about our own processes of discovery regarding the sermons. This is what worked for us. What works for you may be similar—or it may be completely different. The important thing is to dig in.

We encourage you with all our hearts to accept the unique opportunity to be taught by the Prophet Joseph Smith, the man foreordained to open the dispensation of the fulness of times. The spirit in his words flows from his generation to ours, offering rich blessings to those who have eyes to see and ears to hear.

SHERI DEW

VIRGINIA H. PEARCE

INTRODUCTORY ESSAYS

❧❀❧

Virginia H. Pearce
Sheri Dew

ANGELS AND EPIPHANIES

VIRGINIA H. PEARCE

S tanding at the kitchen sink several months ago, with the spring sun warming my face, I had an epiphany. It was a flash of insight: a sudden understanding of my contentment, gratitude, and wonder at being a woman in the restored Church of Jesus Christ of Latter-day Saints. I had walked in the back door a few minutes earlier, returning from the Salt Lake Temple, where I had just been set apart as an ordinance worker. Absently, I turned off the faucet. Wow. I had just been set apart to officiate in sacred ordinances—to help those on both sides of the veil receive God's power through priesthood authority! Short, slightly pudgy, inconsequential me—a middle-aged widow and ordinary mortal—would be in the temple several hours every week, an authorized player in the great drama of the Restoration! How could this be? My wonder could not be contained.

In a sudden flash of enlightenment I saw the importance of my personal path toward the temple and the sacredness of its ordinances. I saw all of my life as a journey to the temple—and the temple as a bridge on my continuing path back to God. Now, that sounds just like church-speak. I don't know how to express that this time I really "got it"!

Drying my hands on a nearby towel, I walked into the other room, powered up my computer, and went to the josephsmithpapers.org site to reread the Minutes of the Female Relief Society of Nauvoo. You see, I had "discovered" those Minutes only a few months before. You may be asking where I have been, but to be perfectly honest, although I go to church every single week, prepare lessons and talks and listen to others do the same, and was familiar with many of the sentences and phrases from Joseph's teachings to the Relief Society, somehow I had never read the Minutes (and, more important, Joseph Smith's words contained in the Minutes) in their entirety until recently.

My flash of insight at the kitchen sink included a surprising look at how many seemingly disparate threads had come together during the past few years to create this unified message about me, my life, and the temple.

Don't you just love the way the Lord always has something "brand-new" to help you learn exactly what you need to know at exactly the right moment? And that is just what the Lord did for me—over and over—as I sought personal revelation to invent a new life following the death of my husband. I had been asking Him, "What should I do with my life now?"

To help me answer this question, He placed specific people in my life—some living and some historical; dozens of conversations—some intense and some casual; various projects and assignments; scriptural insights; lessons and talks in church that went straight to my heart; the new history of Relief Society, *Daughters in My Kingdom*—a plethora of clouds bursting with blessings. But, without doubt, some of the most needful insights came to me through the words of Joseph Smith, carried into my heart by the Holy Ghost.

Gradually, as I studied Joseph's words, my question became two questions: "What do you want me to do?" was still my most pressing question, but surprisingly, there was another: "Who am I, anyway?" I mean, "Who am I outside of my roles as a wife, mother, grandmother, friend?" With the death of my husband, my very identity seemed more fluid.

I suspect those two questions are also ones you grapple with from time to time—no matter your individual circumstances. In fact, I think they must have been critical questions for the women who gathered in the newly formed Female Relief Society of Nauvoo. Joseph's answers blessed their lives just as they continue to bless the life of every faithful woman of this dispensation.

This is not a commentary—just a personal essay, albeit an illustration, of sorts, about how one pretty average person went about studying Joseph's words. I offer it to you, acknowledging that it may be of no greater use than to convince you that another way would be more effective! And I can be quite happy cheering you on in any approach that works for you.

Where do we start when we go to sacred texts to learn? With prayer, of course. We can invite the Holy Ghost to teach us, to enlighten our minds, to help us discern between that which is true and that which is not. He is the grand interpreter and becomes our guide as we seek Him. The voice of the Spirit is a trustworthy voice—and that voice is surely allowed to speak as we use our agency to ask for it.

On first being introduced to Joseph Smith's lectures to the women of Relief Society, I read them through—start to finish—with pencil in hand. I marked anything that caught my attention, anything that puzzled me, anything that seemed to reverberate with personal meaning, anything that was particularly well said. My question marks and exclamation points littered the margins of each page. As I read, I began to formulate questions—questions about specific passages but, more important, questions that were in my heart.

On concluding the first reading, I went back through slowly, poking around at some of the things I had underlined. I considered my question marks and began to do a little research about the historical context of the lectures, hoping to shed light on meaning. What was Joseph alluding to here? Was there something else going on that I didn't know about? Why would he have said this? In short, I wanted to know about Joseph and the people of Nauvoo in the year 1842.

As is the way with revelation, the ideas Joseph Smith elucidates in the Relief Society Minutes are embedded in immediate concerns—some mundane, some sublime, some emotion charged—in this case, concerns that were very much a part of Nauvoo in the year 1842. The revealed principles came to Joseph and to his followers embedded in context, in a "here and now" that may seem strange to us but made sense to those actually living in 1842.

Specifically understanding Nauvoo—in all its complexities—would surely be useful in understanding the application of Joseph Smith's teachings in our twenty-first-century lives. When we can see the historical problem being addressed, we can separate the application from the doctrine-based principle. Only then can we make the leap to apply the principle to our modern lives, enriched but unencumbered by historical circumstances.

For example, when we seek to understand the teachings of Jesus' story of the Good Samaritan, it helps for us to know what place Samaritans held in the context of the New Testament world. Knowing their status elucidates the principle of Christian service—and ultimately Jesus' universal Atonement—more forcefully.

Besides that, this interesting puzzle is fun to untangle! I love to hunt through historical facts and individual lives to find the doctrines that will enrich the truth I already understand and motivate me to apply it in my present circumstances. Taking the template of what I already know to be true, I can assimilate or discard new information.

My ideas for studying may seem sequential and linear. First, you pray; then, you read, and so on. And of course, there is a beginning point, but in reality, it's not quite that orderly. In fact, as you dive deeper and deeper, it all runs together in messy ways. You keep praying. You go down this road, then that, as you look at the historical records. You think of scriptures, you think of more questions, your everyday life pops up, the things you already know to be true deepen into a new understanding, you read a current conference talk or hear a lesson and fit new pieces into the puzzle, and on and on. "Line upon line" sounds so tidy, but learning to me always feels more like "a little right here and a little way over there," a flash here and a stupor there. Maybe, in the service of honesty, I'm disclosing a bit too much about my own personal level of confusion!

IDEAS FOR STUDYING PROPHETIC WRITINGS

- PRAY—SEEK THE GUIDANCE OF THE HOLY GHOST.
- READ STRAIGHT THROUGH, UNDERLINING AND MAKING QUICK NOTES.
- FORMULATE QUESTIONS.
- RETURN TO THE TEXT, PARTICULARLY THE PLACES YOU HAVE MARKED.
- STUDY HISTORICAL CONTEXT.
- IDENTIFY DOCTRINES, PRINCIPLES, AND APPLICATIONS, AND COMPARE AGAINST WHAT YOU ALREADY KNOW TO BE TRUE.
- SEEK A WITNESS AND MAKE PERSONAL APPLICATION.
- ACT OUT OF YOUR NEW OR STRENGTHENED GOSPEL KNOWLEDGE.

As I talk about some of the things I learned from Joseph Smith—about who I am and what I am to do—they may seem all over the map to a perfectly sane reader. But, trust me, at the kitchen sink that morning, they all came together for me, and maybe, just maybe I can explain that all to you—if you can persist through this entire essay! Oh, that I had the voice of an angel . . .

So, what did Joseph have to teach me about who I am and what I am to do?

I learned that I am part of an ancient order of women[1]—a full participant in the Church of Jesus Christ.

Relief Society "is divinely made, divinely authorized, divinely instituted, divinely ordained of God to minister for the salvation of the souls of women and men. Therefore there is not any organization that can compare with it, . . . that can ever occupy the same stand and platform that this can."[2]

Joseph taught that "the Church was never perfectly organized"[3] until we women were part of that structure. The organization of the Relief Society marks the first time in the restored Church that the women were given offices in the formal Church organization. Inclusion like this was uncommon in 1842, when women could not vote and rarely held offices in male-dominated organizations. In fact, "as the nineteenth century began, . . . the personal property of a wife became the property of her husband as soon as he reduced it to possession." Most of the early married women's acts did not appear until the 1840s in the United States.[4] The 1840s were truly the "beginning of better days"[5] for women.

Understanding that I, as a Relief Society sister, am a full-fledged participant in the structure of the Church empowers me to speak responsibly and clearly as I counsel with men in family and Church settings.

I am not on the fringes of this Church, but have the opportunity and responsibility to help solve problems and attend to needs.

Elder M. Russell Ballard has repeatedly taught us about men and women working together, both in Church leadership and in families: "This is the miracle of Church councils: listening to each other and listening to the Spirit! When we support one another in Church councils, we begin to understand how God can take ordinary men and women and make of them extraordinary leaders."[6]

As women, we can work respectfully with the brethren—with confidence and inspiration. I loved the description of the conversation between Joseph Smith, John Taylor, Emma Smith, Sarah Cleveland, and Eliza R. Snow regarding the selection of a name for their society in that first meeting above the red brick store in Nauvoo. The men thought it should be "The Nauvoo Female Benevolent Society." However, the women objected, gave their reasons, and put forth the word *Relief* in the place of *Benevolent*. After hearing their argument, "Elder Taylor arose and said—I shall have to concede the point—your arguments are so potent I cannot stand before them—I shall have to give way—

"Prest J.S. said I also shall have to concede the point, all I shall have to give to the poor, I shall give to this Society."[7]

So I am a confident, inspired, valued, and fully vested member.

I learned, again, the importance of unity.

Unity is a holy thing. How many times did the Savior reiterate His oneness with the Father and His injunction that if we are not one, we are not His? Unity doesn't mean "rubber-stamping" the word of our leaders.

It requires listening, weighing, pondering, seeking inspiration, speaking up, articulating problems, and recommending solutions. It means that when a decision is made in council, all agree to support that decision wholeheartedly. It means we will not hold back or sabotage the final decision, even when it wasn't the one we brought to the table.

Several years ago I was serving in the Young Women organization in my ward. One day in a meeting with the youth leaders the bishop presented us with a program to help the young people read the Book of Mormon. He proposed that we offer a trip the next summer to those who completed the reading. As he continued to talk about it, I felt uneasy and finally decided that I should express my misgivings about the idea. This good bishop listened respectfully and responded to my concerns. We had an open discussion in the meeting. I felt heard, and as we listened to one another, I was suddenly filled with ideas—things I could do personally to support the bishop's decision. As we enthusiastically carried forth in unity with this program we saw abundant blessings in the lives of leaders and parents as well as young people. Looking back, I realized that had I not voiced my concerns—and had the council not considered them—I could easily have sabotaged the whole program, thereby compromising its success and the abundant blessings that came to me as I worked with the other leaders to make it successful.

Joseph said: "all must act in concert or nothing can be done—that the Society should move according to the ancient Priesthood . . ."[8]

Unity of feeling is not just about making decisions, however. Joseph taught that full Christian fellowship, growing from charity, must be sought. "It grieves me that there is no fuller fellowship—if one member suffer all feel it—by union of feeling we obtain pow'r with God."[9] In actuality, we have covenanted with God to "bear one another's burdens ... to mourn with those that mourn, yea, and to comfort those that stand in need of comfort."[10]

Unity depends on our recognizing that each of us has different talents and skills to contribute—different gifts—and that by uniting them, we can function as a whole. In fact, those of us "which seem to be more feeble, are necessary."[11] In his April 28 lecture (the lengthiest one recorded) Joseph read and expounded upon the twelfth chapter of 1 Corinthians, warning against aspiring to offices in the Church, asking "that every person should stand and act in the place appointed, and thus sanctify the Society and get it pure—"[12] In summary, in verse 27 Paul teaches that "ye are the body of Christ, and members in particular." Could there be a more wonderful statement of individuality and unity!

I learned that we, as women, have been blessed with the right and responsibility to expound and teach from the scriptures.

Like Emma Smith, we are "ordain'd ... to expound the scriptures to all; and to teach the female part of the community."[13] One Sunday, not long ago, I taught Relief Society in my ward. The teacher was going to be out of town and I was asked to substitute. I read the material, I thought about its meaning, and I prayed about the sisters in my Relief Society—who are some of my dearest friends on earth. It was a wonderful week. And then Sunday came, and together we discussed gospel truths. I had an opportunity to hear their thoughts and testimonies and to bear witness to those truths myself. It doesn't get any better than that!

I love to discuss the gospel. I don't really care where—in a Primary class, in a Relief Society meeting, on a visiting teaching visit, on a morning walk with friends, or at my computer. There is something about speaking scriptural truth out loud, writing it on a page, or teaching and being taught by faithful, covenant-keeping women that breathes life into me.

Actually, talking out loud is the one way I can really figure out what I think. I know the chatter certainly must be tiresome to others, but it is one clear way I can receive a witness of truth: speak it out loud and the Holy Ghost confirms it, or I can tell right away that what I just said isn't really how it is—and correct myself.

I learned something about my nature as a woman—my inherent strengths and weaknesses.

Not long ago a Relief Society sister called, asking me to take dinner to another sister in our ward. I was thrilled. I truly want to do good, but more often than not, I just don't know who needs help. Or if I know, I don't exactly know how to knock on her door. Joseph was speaking directly to me when he said: "—it is natural for females to have feelings of charity—you are now plac'd in a situation where you can act according to those sympathies which God has planted in your bosoms."[14]

The "situation" you and I have been placed in—where we can act on our feelings of charity, live up to our privileges, and associate with angels—in part must be our front-row seat in Relief Society, as well as in our neighborhoods, in the workplace, and, most sacredly, within the walls of our homes.

In speaking of the Relief Society's charge to help us exercise charity, President Gordon B. Hinckley asked the rhetorical question, "Who, even in the wildest stretch of imagination, can fathom the uncountable acts of charity that have been performed, the food that has been put on barren tables, the faith that has been nurtured in desperate hours of illness, the wounds that have been bound up, the pains that have been ameliorated by loving hands and quiet and reassuring words, the comfort that has been extended in times of death and consequent loneliness?"[15]

I can't stop thinking about the ramifications of Joseph's statement that "it is natural for females to have feelings of charity." I've seen that pure love extended time and time again from my sisters. I have felt it myself. And when we are in possession of true charity, life is ever so good. We see nobility in every person; every situation seems worthwhile; we feel energetically able and up to our tasks. Being filled with charity is being filled with the Spirit of the Lord. True charity is His gift to those who pray earnestly for it and live with the overriding desire to follow Him.[16] Taking dinner to someone in need can certainly be an expression of charity—an expression of the pure love of Christ. But true charity is much more than an action, although it is the motivator for truly benevolent actions.[17] However, as we serve others and give of ourselves, we increase the likelihood that we will be successful in developing true charity.

In Nauvoo there were plenty of opportunities for the women to exercise charity. We cannot forget the daily lives of people building a city from a swamp, assimilating new citizens on an almost daily basis, many from foreign countries, sometimes unskilled, and most often without monetary resources. The women were consumed with the tasks of providing and preparing food and shelter; responding to birth, death, and sickness; and participating in the ever-present web of social and familial connections. It was a city bustling with the expected activities of daily living on the frontiers of nineteenth-century America.

But beyond these activities, there were some extraordinary events and conditions peculiar to that particular time and place and people. And it seemed that these events often called for the "pure love of Christ." These events would call for exercising charity in an absence of clear information. They would require charitable faith in leaders, charitable forgiveness toward those who maligned Joseph unfairly. These events also sometimes drew out the negative proclivities in the women—their tendency (and ours) to be overzealous, judgmental, and self-righteous.

The year 1842 saw difficult forces at work both in and out of the Church. John C. Bennett's name dominates this struggle. John C. Bennett was a charismatic convert who helped Joseph Smith to found Nauvoo. He was its first mayor, as well as major general in the Nauvoo Legion. However, his character proved to be unsavory. He seduced one woman after another by telling them Joseph was secretly teaching that illicit sexual intercourse was acceptable if kept secret. Calling it "spiritual wifery," he used Joseph's teachings about plural marriage as a scheme for tricking women and indulging his own sexual appetite. When confronted with the unsavory rumors and accusations, he repeatedly pled for forgiveness and begged Joseph not to expose him. He signed affidavits and testified that "any one who has said that I have stated that General Joseph Smith has given me authority to hold illicit intercourse with women is a Liar in the face of God."[18] Joseph wanted to believe in Bennett's reformation. However, despite his public statements, Bennett continued his sinful behavior, until Joseph finally spoke openly about his misdeeds.

Bennett was excommunicated on May 25. Humiliated and angry, he left Nauvoo and began to gather and inflame the enemies of the Church. Traveling from city to city, he lectured against the Mormons, published a book, and wrote numerous letters to newspapers. Bennett also worked to create dissension within the Church, poisoning, at least temporarily, Orson Pratt, Sidney Rigdon, and George W. Robinson, as well as others.

Bennett was successful in rallying some to his cause because his accusations played upon the lack of accurate information regarding the doctrine and practice of plural marriage. Those who were practicing it (Joseph and some of the Twelve) did so privately, which gave rise to confusion and susceptibility to untrue rumors.[19]

And so, the confusion about plural marriage, coupled with the accusations and behavior of John C. Bennett and others, forms the historical context that gave rise to some of Joseph's recurring themes to the women of Relief Society. He continually admonished them to be merciful and full of charity—to refrain from self-righteousness and gossip. "As females possess refin'd feelings and sensitivenes[s]; they are also subject to an overmuch zeal . . . [which causes] them to be rigid in a religious capacity—should be arm'd with mercy notwithstanding the iniquity among us."[20]

But knowing the particular circumstances prompting Joseph's warnings doesn't invalidate the principles he taught and their applicability to us. I am motivated to strive for more charity when I hear him say: "let your hearts expand—let them be enlarged towards others—you must be longsuff'ring and bear with the faults and errors of mankind," further warning that "the female part of the community are apt to be contracted in their views. You must not be contracted, but you must be liberal in your feelings."[21]

You may feel inclined, as I did, to underline those words when you read the Minutes, since we women find ourselves far too often discussing others with less than liberal feelings. Joseph teaches me, warns me, that this is something I am apt to do. Recognizing this, I am armed to make a choice to stop, to pray to be filled with charity and to enlarge my heart toward those whom I might have judged and criticized.

In the last stage of my husband's illness, he wore a mask over his mouth and nose to enable him to breathe more easily. He depended on others to situate the mask properly so that the air forced through it didn't escape and blow into his eyes. One morning, for whatever reason, I was having difficulty fitting the mask successfully. I thought I was doing what I had always done, and then he would signal that it wasn't working. I tried again and again as he waited patiently, and I became slightly frustrated. I finally got it right, and just as I turned to attend to something else, he said something. I couldn't understand him, and he repeated it. Still unable to understand him through the mask, I took it off, only to find that he just wanted to thank me. Of course, now I had to go through the frustration of trying to get it on right yet again! The amazing part of this little tale is not my frustration and annoyance, but Jim's interpretation and reaction to it. He didn't say anything immediately, but when the nurse came that afternoon, he asked her—with great effort—to "help Ginny with the mask. She's losing her confidence."

That interpretation and response, I believe, is what true charity looks like. Rather than be offended and hurt by my behavior, he interpreted my actions as having come from a place of ignorance rather than flawed character. When we are filled with charity, we understand that the behavior of others is most often motivated by their desires to do good, even when that is not the reality of their actions. President Thomas S. Monson articulates it well: "I have in mind the charity that impels us to be sympathetic, compassionate, and merciful, not only in times of sickness and affliction and distress but also in times of weakness or error on the part of others."[22]

When we give a charitable response to someone, rather than an accusatory or defensive one, we inspire and motivate others to open their hearts and try harder to make things right. True charity in our everyday encounters with one another leads to everyday miracles!

Charity is a necessity, and Joseph honors us when he speaks forthrightly. He doesn't tiptoe around in condescending ways. He treats us as responsible, mature agents who have the power to repent and do better.

"Sisters of this Society, shall there be strife among you? I will not have it—you must repent and get the love of God. Away with selfrighteousness."[23] I find his chastisement more respectful and motivating than many of the laudatory speeches we often hear as women.

I came to appreciate more fully the reality that we are each in a mortal moment—with a premortal history behind us and a glorious future ahead.

In striving to understand Joseph and his world better, I learned that the book of Abraham was published in the *Times and Seasons* in March 1842. Begun in 1835, it is a unique piece of what would become canonized scripture. In the words of Richard Bushman, "Only Joseph Smith wrote a pre-earth history of God and then filled out humanity's future in the expanding universe."[24] Intelligences, light and truth, and the burden of earth life experience filled its pages: "We will prove them herewith, to see if they will do all things whatsoever the Lord their God shall command them."[25] Once again we see 1842 in the larger context of eternity—a mortal moment with an eternity before and an eternity stretching into the future. And is that not what we each live in? This awareness colors *every* thought about who I am and what I am to do!

I think about the to-do lists we each carry with us and am not advocating that we get rid of them. But I think more about how prayerful I can be in making the list, and how prayerful I can be about how I carry it out. Can I see that whatever I do can, in reality, be done for my eternal good? When I wash the dishes and do the laundry, do I see those mundane tasks as ways to create environments of cleanliness and order where the Spirit of the Lord can dwell? Do I see them as offerings to those I love? As a way to respond to the divinity within me that loves peace and light and order? Running errands for someone, listening, touching, affirming, encouraging—this is the holiness of life.

What woman cannot respond eagerly to President Henry B. Eyring's statement: "The promise to you and me in the last days is that after seeking God and serving his children with unwearyingness, we will come to know his will. The promise is not just that I will have the power to do what's on my list of tasks but that I will know what to put there. On those occasions when I have known what should be there, I've found myself glancing at the list as a source of joy, not anxiety."[26]

I learned, again, of the sweetness, as well as the complexity of marriage relationships.

As we study Joseph's words to the women of the Female Relief Society of Nauvoo, we cannot help but think of Emma. In that first meeting on March 17 she is elected president.[27] She chooses as counselors Mrs. Sarah M. Cleveland and Mrs. Elizabeth Ann Whitney. They were given the right to "preside just as the Presidency preside over the church; and if they need his instruction—ask him, he will give it from time to time . . . He [Elder Taylor] then laid his hands on the head of Mrs. Smith and blessed her, and confirm'd upon her all the blessings which had been confer'd on her [referring to D&C 25], that she might . . . possess all the qualifications necessary for her to stand and preside and dignify her Office, to teach the females those principles requisite for their future usefulness."[28]

The year 1842 would be one of great difficulty for Emma. But it is one in which prophecies concerning her would come to fruition and in which we see her intellect and loyalty exercised on behalf of her husband and the Church.

Just a little over a month before the Relief Society was organized, Emma gave birth to a son who did not live. Another baby, Don Carlos, had died of malaria the previous August. These were the fourth and fifth children Emma had lost. Emma's mother, Elizabeth Hale, died on February 16, 1841; her father, Isaac Hale, had died three years earlier. Surely this was a woman worn down by death and heartache.

An attempted assassination of Lilburn Boggs, the former governor of Missouri, occurred on May 6, 1842. John C. Bennett saw it as another opportunity to bring Joseph down. He named Orrin Porter Rockwell, who was in the area at the time, as the assassin acting under the direction of Joseph Smith. Missouri issued an extradition order for Joseph and Rockwell. From August to December, Joseph would be moving from place to place—slipping in and out of Nauvoo, meeting friends and Emma as they came to him by circuitous routes and in secret. His letters betray a deep sense of loneliness and uncertainty. In spite of the danger, Emma's fragile health throughout the fall brought Joseph back to Nauvoo repeatedly.

During this time, Joseph relied heavily upon Emma's judgment, business skills, comfort, and support. She repeatedly petitioned Illinois Governor Thomas Carlin on Joseph's behalf. The correspondence between them is an indication that "she was a woman of extraordinary ability and temperament who understood the finer points of the complex issue and articulated an intelligent argument. Carlin himself . . . 'expressed astonishment at the judgment and talent manifest in the manner of her address' after reading her first letter."[29]

Emma's letters to Joseph often spoke of business concerns: property that she had sold, questions regarding various business transactions, efforts to clear debts, and so forth.[30]

Her loving loyalty and tireless efforts on his behalf were just as real as her personal anguish over the doctrine of plural marriage must have been. Joseph's love for and dependence on her must have been constantly at odds with the mandate he had received from God—and dared not disobey—to be sealed to plural wives.

Now, I am not suggesting that my marriage relationship or yours is as complicated as Joseph and Emma's. But our marriages are not simple either. Being yoked to another human being in this mortal world requires charity. It requires patience, humility, forgiveness, repentance, and a host of other Christian virtues. As outside pressures ebb and flow, these virtues come under added stress. Joseph teaches us "how to act towards husbands to treat them with mildness and affection. When a man is borne down with trouble—when he is perplex'd, if he can meet a smile, not an argument—if he can meet with mildness, it will calm down his soul and soothe his feelings. When the mind is going to despair, it needs a solace."[31]

I love those words when applied to the sacred opportunity between a husband and wife—to sense despair and give solace, to soothe, to offer mildness. In our society, men often feel constrained to always seem strong, to never look as if they feel inadequate, to talk as if no mountain is too steep or too difficult. But in the sacredness of a covenant relationship, a man's perplexities and troubles—even despair—can find expression. And it is our supreme privilege to reassure, support, and offer our undying love and loyalty.

I learned, again, about my inseparable connection to the priesthood.

I am not offended when someone offers the explanation that "the men get the priesthood and the women get to bear children," as if there were separate prizes being passed out. But that explanation doesn't really resonate with me either. I feel too clearly the power and blessings of the priesthood in *everything* I do. I appreciate those who hold the priesthood—who have been given the authority to offer the blessings of the priesthood to worthy mortals—and have done so and continue to do so for me personally. But I feel that I too participate in the priesthood. Let me try to explain.

I have heard all my life about the sense of deprivation of those who "don't have priesthood" in their homes. Obviously, they are referring to the fact that there is not a holder of the priesthood in the home—a worthy, ordained male.

When my husband died and I faced living alone, that was something I thought about. From the time of my birth, I had lived in a home presided over by a worthy priesthood holder—first my father, and then my husband. I had always felt secure. I had always felt cared for. I had always felt protected. What would become of those feelings?

It's true that I miss the availability of one who holds the priesthood.

It is so convenient to have a husband who can readily offer blessings. But I have been blessed abundantly by the necessity to invite a home teacher or a son or a son-in-law to give me blessings. My relationships with them have only been enriched by those experiences.

Beyond that, for me, one of the stunningly powerful discoveries of living alone is the absolutely overwhelming sense I have of being protected and cared for. I feel the Lord's presence in every corner of my home. I feel His power in every decision of my life. I feel guided and comforted and loved. Now, what is this if it is not what has come to me because of the power of the priesthood—His power? I believe He is available and present in my life because of the covenants I have been privileged to make—first in the waters of baptism and finally within the walls of holy temples.

A man, speaking of his divorced mother said, "Her greatest strength came from the Lord Himself. She did not have to wait for a visit [from priesthood holders] in order to have the blessings of the priesthood in her home, and when visitors left, those blessings did not leave with them. Because she was faithful to the covenants she had made in the waters of baptism and in the temple, she always had the blessings of the priesthood in her life."[32]

"The priesthood" isn't the congregation of men who meet together each Sunday, although we sometimes refer to them that way. The priesthood is, in essence, God's power. It is the power by which the worlds were created. It is the power by which our bodies were created and which allows those bodies to create offspring. It is the power by which we are washed clean of our sins and are given the gift of the Holy Ghost. It is the power by which we experience forgiveness from God and partake of Christ's atoning sacrifice. It is the power with which we are actually endowed in sacred temples. It is the power by which we are sealed as eternal companions with the possibility of eternal increase, the power to eventually inherit all that the Father hath.[33]

Priesthood, truly, is a power beyond my comprehension. I believe I have "it" in my home.

On my first reading of the Minutes, one of the paragraphs I marked was in the April 28 meeting. It concerned an issue raised by members of the Relief Society in those early meetings: the question of whether it was proper for women to anoint and bless others. This clearly seems like a question about the priesthood. That is obviously the way Joseph saw it too. His journal of April 28, 1842, states: "at Two o'clock after-noon met the members of the 'Female relief Society' and . . . Gave a lecture on the pries[t]hood shewing how the Sisters would come in possession of the priviliges & blesings and gifts of the priesthood—& that the signs should follow them. such as healing the sick casting out devils &c. & that they might attain unto. these blessings. by a virtuous life & conversation & diligence in keeping all the commandments."[34]

So what did I do with this question? I read and reread the entire April 28 lecture—prayerfully. I thought about the doctrine of the priesthood—the things I already knew. I thought about my absolute conviction that we are led by prophets today and realized that I had never heard them talk about women anointing and blessing the sick, so evidently it was no longer sanctioned. I began to look at historical sources, read and reread some recent general conference talks on priesthood, read and reread scriptures about the priesthood, particularly in the Doctrine and Covenants. In all of this studying, which was by no means exhaustive, I happened onto a paper entitled "Female Ritual Healing in Mormonism." In it, the authors trace the practice of healing by women in the Church—from before Nauvoo through the twentieth century. They show that the practice of women giving healing blessings gradually gave way to the modern era of codification, when many practices were made uniform and authorized to be performed only within dedicated temples.[35] I began to understand more clearly the evolution of application.

No matter the differences in application, however, I believe that the doctrine and principles behind the practice in 1842 operate just as forcefully today. They include accessing God's power through faith, virtue, and worthiness. I am a witness that the prayer of faith coupled with worthiness in covenant-keeping women produces miracles as surely today as it did in 1842.

Compilers of Joseph's words, in discussing the question of propriety of women laying hands on others, state: "At this meeting [April 28], however, the Prophet explained that this [practice of administering] was entirely appropriate. He sympathized with those who did not understand his larger vision of the situation. He said 'that the time had not been before, that these things could be in their proper order—that the Church is not now organized in its proper order, and cannot be until the Temple is completed.' In the Temple women would with oil and by the laying on of the hands confer on their sisters blessings of greater eternal significance than the beautiful but single effect of healing an illness."[36]

I learned, again, about the supreme importance of the temple and its ordinances.

The year 1842 began with great hope—at least from Joseph's pen. The basement of the Nauvoo Temple was completed, and baptisms for the dead would shortly begin to be performed in the new font. Joseph's journal entry of January 6, 1842, describes his excitement as he looks forward to the completion of the Nauvoo Temple and its overarching meaning in terms of restoring the fulness of the gospel—the restoration of *all* principles and practices of the ancient prophets.[37]

On first reading the Minutes, I thought very little about the temple as a meaningful force in the early Relief Society, even though I knew that the initial idea for forming a society had come from a desire on the part of the women to sew shirts for those who were working on the temple.[38]

I began to believe, however, as I studied additional records from Nauvoo, that in Joseph Smith's thinking, the organization of Relief Society, the institution of baptisms for the dead,[39] and the practice of plural marriage were all part of this grand restitution of the fulness of the gospel in preparation for the millennial reign of the Savior. After all, Joseph referred to his time as "a day in which all things are concurring to bring about the completion of the fullness of the Gospel, a fullness of the dispensation of dispensations, even the fullness of times . . ."[40]

Joseph gave the temple endowment for the first time in this dispensation to nine men on May 4, 1842. As we look at that date and the date of his lectures to the Relief Society, it is easy to conclude that much of what Joseph taught was intended to help them prepare to participate worthily in temple ordinances. Emma would receive her temple endowment the following year, in September of 1843. Others would follow. "As the [Nauvoo] temple neared completion, 36 women were called to serve as temple ordinance workers."[41]

Sister Julie B. Beck, general Relief Society president, takes us to Nauvoo in 1842: "We can imagine what it must have been like for the sisters to be in Joseph Smith's Red Brick Store at those first Relief Society Meetings, facing the hill where a temple was being built as the Prophet taught them that 'there should be a select society, separate from all the evils of the world, choice, virtuous, and holy.'"[42]

The idea of "worthiness" as a requirement for membership in the Female Relief Society of Nauvoo seems strange. In today's Church, there is no worthiness requirement for participation in Relief Society. But worthiness is critical to participating in temple blessings. So I believe that points additionally to the thought that Joseph felt that one of the primary purposes of Relief Society was to prepare women to receive and administer temple blessings. We are to be worthy, "separate from all the evils of the world, choice, virtuous and holy."[43] "All hearts must repent—be pure."[44]

By April of 1842 the temple walls were rising. "The sound of the polisher's chisel—converting the rude stone of the quarry into an artful shape—sent forth its busy hum: all were busily employed—the work was fast progressing."[45] William W. Player came from England in June and became the principal stone setter. The need for lumber was finally solved when a mission was sent to the pineries in Wisconsin. The first lumber arrived in August, allowing the framing to begin. "'A cheering assemblage of wagons, horses, oxen and men . . . began with zeal and gladness to pull the raft to pieces and haul it up to the Temple,' where 'a large assemblage of carpenters, joiners, etc. . . . succeeded in preparing the lumber and laying the joists.'"[46]

On October 30 the first meeting was held on the main floor in the temple, on a temporary floor with seats fixed. By the end of the year the temple walls were four feet high. The dream of a temple once again was being made real. In this temple, the full endowment would be offered. To men. And to women. And together they would be sealed in the new and everlasting covenant, eligible to be heirs of all that the Father hath, "armed with thy power, and that thy name may be upon them, and thy glory be round about them, and thine angels have charge over them . . ."[47]

Millennial in scope and eternal in its realities, in my mind, this vision of the temple and what it means illuminates every sentence Joseph uttered to the women of the Female Relief Society of Nauvoo. I have come to believe that a serious reader of the Relief Society Minutes cannot separate the temple with its implications from her understanding of women and our divine mission. In fact, I believe that only as we come to understand the temple and its ordinances are we able to shed light on our divine identity and purpose. I have found it a useful exercise to read all of Joseph's words, thinking of how each idea is connected to temple preparation and participation. Without reservation, I recommend this experience to you.

And that takes me back to my epiphany at the kitchen sink last spring. Who I am and what I am to do suddenly had everything to do with the temple—not about how often I should go or anything so simple. It is about living up to my privileges—the privileges offered in the house of the Lord. It is about the centrality of the temple to my mortal life, its importance as the place where I can go to "feel" what God wants to teach me. It is about the dignity with which I leave the temple—"armed with power." It is about the way Joseph saw the women of The Church of Jesus Christ of Latter-day Saints—the sisters in 1842 as well as the one I look at in the mirror each morning.

Like a wave of warmth and light, knowledge washed over me: knowledge that my life is just a moment between the premortal and post-mortal eternities; knowledge that I belong to the kingdom of God on earth, with an opportunity to participate fully; knowledge that I have inherent spiritual gifts, as well as weaknesses; knowledge that my marriage relationship will go on through the eternities; knowledge that priesthood power is present in my life as I strive for more purity; knowledge that as I live up to my privileges, angels cannot be restrained;[48] and knowledge that truth is eminently available in the house of the Lord.

Who am I? I am a woman of God, a woman of covenant. What am I to do? Live up to my privileges.

I believe the answers to those questions might be the same for you. Read Joseph's words. Pray about them. Study them. And expect angels and epiphanies.

Notes

1. *Daughters in My Kingdom* (Salt Lake City: The Church of Jesus Christ of Latter-day Saints, 2011), 1, quoting Eliza R. Snow: "Although the name may be of modern date, the institution is of ancient origin. We were told by our martyred prophet that the same organization existed in the church anciently."

2. Joseph F. Smith, as quoted by Gordon B. Hinckley, *Discourses of President Gordon B. Hinckley*, 2 vols. (Salt Lake City: Deseret Book, 2005–2006), 1:185–86.

3. *Teachings of Presidents of the Church: Joseph Smith* (Salt Lake City: The Church of Jesus Christ of Latter-day Saints, 2007), 451.

4. Richard H. Chused, "Married Women's Property Law: 1800–1850," *The Georgetown Law Journal*, 1983, 71:1359, 1361.

5. *Nauvoo Relief Society Minute Book* (hereafter *Minutes*), April 28, 1842. Available online at http://josephsmithpapers.org/paperDetails/nauvoo-relief-society-minute-book?dm=image -and-text&zm=zoom-inner&tm=expanded&p=1&s=&sm=none.

6. M. Russell Ballard, "Counseling with Our Councils," *Ensign*, May 1994, 26.

7. *Minutes*, March 17, 1842.

8. *Minutes*, March 30, 1842.

9. *Minutes*, June 9, 1842.

10. Mosiah 18:8–9.

11. 1 Corinthians 12:22.

12. *Minutes*, April 28, 1842.

13. *Minutes*, March 17, 1842, wherein Joseph refers to Section 25 given concerning Emma (and all women).

14. *Minutes*, April 28, 1842.

15. Gordon B. Hinckley, "Ambitious to Do Good," *Ensign*, March 1992, 4.

16. Moroni 7:41.

17. " . . . the pure love of Christ. It is never used to denote alms or deeds or benevolence, although it may be a prompting motive" (Bible Dictionary, s.v. "Charity," 632).

18. Richard L. Bushman, *Rough Stone Rolling* (New York: Knopf, 2005), 461.

19. There obviously isn't space in this essay to discuss polygamy—something that is difficult for any of us to understand. I recently read *Women of Faith in the Latter Days, Vol. I: 1775–1820*, edited by Richard E.Turley Jr. and Brittany A. Chapman (Salt Lake City: Deseret Book, 2011). It is a book containing brief biographies and writings of thirty-five women of the early Restoration. It is not a treatise on polygamy, but I was surprised to note that when I finished reading their stories, I felt that I had a clearer understanding of polygamy than I have ever had before. I recommend it for that reason and, of course, for many other reasons.

20. *Minutes*, May 26, 1842.

21. *Minutes*, April 28, 1842.

22. *Teachings of Thomas S. Monson* (Salt Lake City: Deseret Book, 2011), 37.

23. *Minutes*, June 9, 1842.

24. Bushman, *Rough Stone Rolling*, 458.

25. Abraham 3:25.

26. Henry B. Eyring, "Child of Promise," *New Era*, August 1993, 9.

27. The March 17 Minutes indicate that Joseph Smith read the revelation (D&C 25) aloud, stating that Emma was "ordain'd at the time, the Revelation was given, to expound the scriptures to all; and to teach the female part of community; . . ."

28. *Minutes*, March 17, 1842.

29. Andrew H. Hedges and Alex D. Smith, "1842: Joseph Smith, John C. Bennett, and the Extradition Attempt," in *Joseph Smith, the Prophet and Seer,* edited by Richard Neitzel Holzapfel and Kent P. Jackson (Salt Lake City: Deseret Book, 2010), 459.

30. See, for example, this letter written to Joseph in August 1842:

"Dear husband,

"I am ready to go with you if you are obliged to leave; and Hyrum says he will go with me. I shall make the best arrangements I can and be as well prepared as possible. But still I feel good confidence that you can be protected without leaving this country. There is more ways than one to take care of you, and I believe that you can still direct in your business concerns if we are all of us prudent in the matter. If it was pleasant weather I should contrive to see you this evening, but I dare not run to[o] much of a risk on account of so many going to see you. General [James] Adams sends the propositions concerning his land, two dollars an acre, payments as follows, Assumption of Mortgage say about fourteen hundred, interest included. Taxes due, supposed about thirty dollars. Town property one thousand dollars. Balance, Money, payable in one, two, three and four years. Brother Derby will tell you all the information we have on hand. I think we will have news from Quincy as soon as tomorrow.

"Yours affectionately forever

"Emma Smith." (*The Joseph Smith Papers: Journals, Volume 2: December 1841–April 1843* [Salt Lake City: The Church Historian's Presss, 2011], 110–11.)

31. *Minutes*, April 28, 1842.

32. *Daughters in My Kingdom,* 138.

33. See D&C 84:38.

34. *The Joseph Smith Papers: Journals, Vol. 2,* 52.

35. Jonathan A. Stapley and Kristine Wright, "Female Ritual Healing in Mormonism," *Journal of Mormon History,* Winter 2011, 1–85.

36. Andrew F. Ehat and Lyndon W. Cook, *The Words of Joseph Smith* (Salt Lake City: Bookcraft, 1980), 140 fn.

37. As Joseph Smith's journal entry on January 6, 1842, states: "The New Year has been

ushered in and continued thus far under the most favorable auspices. and the Saints seem to be influenced by a kind and indulgent Providence in their disposition & [blessed with] means; to rear the Temple of the most High God, anxiously looking forth to the completion thereof. as an event of the greatest importance to the Church & the world, Making the Saints in Zion to rejoice, and the Hypocrite & Sinner to tremble, Truly this is a day long to be remembered. by. the saints of the Last Days; A day in which the God of heaven has began to restore the ancient <order> of his Kingdom unto. his servants & his people: a day in which all things are concurring together to bring about the compl[e]tion of the fullness of the gospel, a fulness of the dispensation of Dispensations even the fulness of Times; a day in which God has began to make manifest & set in order in his church those things which have been, and those things, which the ancient prophets and wise men desired to see.—but deid [died] without beholding it. a day in which those things begin to be made manifest which have been hid from <before> the foundations of the world. & which Jehovah has promised should be made known in his own due time. unto his servants, to prepare. the earth for the return of his glory, even a celestial glory; and a kingdom of Priests & Kings to God & the Lamb . . . which should come to pass. in the Restitution of all things" (*The Joseph Smith Papers: Journals, Vol. 2*, 25–26).

38. Sarah M. Kimball, "Auto-biography," *The Woman's Exponent*, Vol. 12, no. 7 (September 1, 1883): 51.

39. During the time when Joseph was in hiding (September 1842) he wrote two letters giving specific instructions regarding baptisms for the dead, including the importance of a recorder, the symbolic significance of baptism (death and resurrection), the principle of binding on earth and in heaven through the power and authority of the priesthood, and the teaching that individuals cannot be made perfect without their dead. These letters are designated as sections 127 and 128 of the Doctrine and Covenants. Joseph takes occasion in the letters to explain why he has left Nauvoo, to reassure his creditors that his business debts will be handled, and to ask that the Saints redouble their work on the temple, despite persecution.

40. *Teachings of Presidents of the Church: Joseph Smith* (Salt Lake City: The Church of Jesus Christ of Latter-day Saints, 2007), 510.

41. *Daughters in My Kingdom*, 133.

42. Julie B. Beck, "What I Hope My Granddaughters (and Grandsons) Will Understand about Relief Society," *Ensign*, November 2011, 111.

43. *Minutes*, March 30, 1842.

44. *Minutes*, April 28, 1842.

45. In Don F. Colvin, *The Nauvoo Temple: A Story of Faith* (Provo, UT: BYU, 2002), 22.

46. In Colvin, *The Nauvoo Temple*, 22–23.

47. D&C 109:22.

48. *Minutes*, April 28, 1842.

WHAT JOSEPH SMITH TAUGHT WOMEN
And Why It Matters

❧❀❧

S H E R I   D E W

If I were identifying major themes in my life, one of them would have to be Relief Society, though when I was called in my early twenties to serve as the Relief Society president of a young adult ward, I was flabbergasted. Nothing about me matched my image of a Relief Society leader. "I don't bake bread, I can't quilt, I love sports," I stammered, listing everything that would surely disqualify me. But the bishop said the Lord had spoken, and that was that.

Attending to the varied and often emotionally charged needs of two hundred young-adult-age women trying to find themselves was eye-opening, around-the-clock work. But it gave me a front-row seat from which to watch the Lord work miracle after miracle in the lives of His daughters. It was at that young age that I began to experience the power of a woman's faith. And it was when I began to see that there was a lot more to Relief Society than met the eye.

Fast-forward a decade. My thirties were filled with lots of Church service but also escalating frustration. I had kept a stiff upper lip about not yet marrying, but by thirty-five, I'd lost my sense of humor about everyone (all of my siblings, most of my friends) getting married except me and had become deeply discouraged about it all. In addition to my longing for a companion, the window on my bearing children was narrowing, and the fear that I might never have children was closing its icy grip around me. I spent a lot of time on my knees and in the temple pleading for a family of my own. I couldn't understand why I was being denied such a righteous desire, nor could I sustain a feeling of peace.

Ironically, it was then that I was called to serve as the Relief Society president in a stake comprised almost entirely of young families—in other words, a stake filled with women living the life I wanted. Because my life was different from theirs, I set out to build a bridge between my singleness and their lives filled with family. I prayed a lot, combed the scriptures, and practically took up residence in the temple seeking guidance on how to serve, relate to, and lead my sisters.

One day when I felt stymied about a message I was to deliver at a stake women's conference, I started looking through materials I'd collected while serving a few years earlier on the Relief Society general board under President Barbara Winder. There, buried in a file, was my copy of the Minutes of the Female Relief Society of Nauvoo (hereafter Minutes). I had studied them while serving on the general board, quoted from them, and then filed them when I'd been released.

But on that day, the Minutes that Eliza R. Snow had recorded of the first Relief Society meetings and then packed across the plains reached through a century and a half and spoke to me. I began to read, underline, and scrawl notes in the margins. In particular, I was captivated by the centerpieces of those Minutes—six sermons the Prophet Joseph Smith delivered to the sisters between March and August of 1842.

I had read these documents before—I had even quoted from them—but somehow it had never lodged in my mind that there was a record of sermons Joseph Smith had delivered specifically to women.

At this point, let me ask the obvious: Does what the Prophet Joseph taught a relatively small group of Latter-day Saint women 170 years ago matter now?

I believe his teachings and counsel to women have never mattered more.

Joseph Smith is the Prophet entrusted with ushering in this final dispensation—the man John Taylor said did more "save Jesus only, for the salvation of men in this world, than any other man."[1] Joseph not only saw the Father and the Son but was, as President George Q. Cannon explained, "visited constantly by angels. . . . He had vision after vision in order that his mind might be fully saturated with a knowledge of the things of God."[2] This is the man who declared that if you "gaze into heaven five minutes, you would know more than you would by reading all that ever was written on the subject."[3] It is the man who on another occasion said of one vision in particular, "I could explain a hundred fold more than I ever have of the glories of the kingdoms manifested to me in the vision, were I permitted, and were the people prepared to receive them."[4]

Do you and I want to know what the Prophet of the Restoration—the Prophet tutored constantly by heavenly messengers—taught the women of Nauvoo and thus all women of this dispensation? Surely the answer is a resounding yes!

May I suggest that there is a second reason the Prophet's sermons hold meaning for us today. President Joseph F. Smith declared that the Relief Society holds a unique place in the Lord's Church: "This is . . . the oldest auxiliary organization of the Church and it is of the first importance. It has not only to deal with the necessities of the poor, the sick and the needy, but a part of its duty—and the larger part, too—is to look after the spiritual welfare and salvation of the mothers and daughters of Zion; to see that none is neglected, but that all are guarded against misfortune, calamity, the powers of darkness, and the evils that threaten them in the world. It is the duty of the Relief Societies to look after the spiritual welfare of themselves and of all the female members of the Church."[5]

The Prophet Joseph clearly signaled the Relief Society's vital commission in building faith and testimony among latter-day women and their families. The subjects he covered in his sermons to the sisters of Nauvoo reflect a breathtaking breadth, depth, and doctrinal density. Four of his recurring themes in particular have commanded my interest since that memorable day twenty-plus years ago: first, the place of women in the Lord's kingdom; second, the priesthood; third, the temple; and fourth, charity and the divine nature of women.

My hope is that a brief review of what the Prophet Joseph taught on these themes, along with a few reflections, will whet your appetite to study his words for yourself. We have been admonished to "seek learning even by study and also by faith."[6] Your insights will be far more relevant and meaningful to you than are mine. My promise is that a study of the Prophet's teachings to women will yield rich spiritual rewards.

THE PLACE OF WOMEN IN THE KINGDOM OF GOD

What Is the Significance of What the Prophet Said and Did?

When he set the time and place for the meeting where the Relief Society would be organized, the Prophet Joseph promised the women, "I will organize the women under the priesthood after the pattern of the priesthood."[7] John Taylor, who attended the inaugural meeting with Joseph, declared that the Prophet organized the women "according to the law of Heaven."[8]

After organizing the Relief Society, Joseph stated that "the Church was never perfectly organized until the women were thus organized."[9] He then patterned the new Relief Society presidency like all other presidencies in the Church—after the First Presidency.

That Joseph managed to organize the Relief Society at all was remarkable. These were not carefree days for the Prophet. He was contending with an endless parade of threats from his opponents and accusers, ministering to a growing band of beleaguered Saints and immigrants, attempting to build a temple with meager resources, and leading a young Church through the intense, line-upon-line process of restoration.

Further, this was 1842. Society was highly patriarchal and, as such, strictly limiting of women's rights. Women couldn't vote. (The landmark Seneca Falls Convention, where the push for women's suffrage largely began, was still six years away.) Most weren't formally educated. Few had any way of earning money. And it was still unusual and often difficult for women to own property. Bottom line? In 1842, many still viewed women as being just a rung or two higher on the social ladder than prisoners or slaves.

So it was in contrast to the conventions of the day for the leader of an organization to give women equal time and attention. And yet, not only did Joseph organize the Relief Society and attend regularly, he often took other Church leaders with him: Brigham Young, John Taylor, Heber C. Kimball, Willard Richards, and George A. Smith, to name a few. The Church's presiding leaders found the women worth their time.

Some skeptics have suggested that it took too long (twelve years from the organization of the Church in 1830) to organize the women in 1842. But that perspective is narrow at best. The "restoration of all things" was not simple, formulaic, neat and tidy, or quick.[10] Think of it— the Prophet Joseph was a young adult (just twenty-four years old) when the Church was organized. He had never had a bishop, never been in a quorum, never attended seminary, never had a priesthood leader to nurture him along, never heard a prophet speak. He *was* the prophet. He had no precedent, no manuals, no handbook of instructions. He had to translate the Book of Mormon and then find a way to get it published.

All of the revelations expounding doctrine that we turn to so readily and easily in the Doctrine and Covenants, *he* had to receive. And everything he accomplished was against a backdrop of persistent opposition, persecution, and upheaval.

The Restoration took time, line upon line. It was, and is, ongoing.[11] Counselors to Joseph Smith were not even called until 1832, the First Presidency was not organized until a year later, and the Quorum of the Twelve not until 1835. The first endowments were given in 1842, but vicarious endowments for the dead did not commence until January 1877 in the St. George Temple. So, despite the centrality to the plan of salvation of sealing generations, it took nearly fifty years from the organization of the Church for all the saving ordinances for the dead to be implemented.[12]

Considering the Saints' constant state of upheaval, the line-upon-line nature of the Restoration, and prevailing societal patriarchy, it is nothing short of incredible that the women were organized at all. If Joseph Smith had been taking his cues from his circumstances or from the world, he most likely wouldn't have bothered. But he was taking direction from the Lord.

Elder James E. Talmage declared that "the world's greatest champion of woman and womanhood is Jesus the Christ."[13] The Prophet Joseph was a reflection of the Master he served. He demonstrated by what he said and did that women are vital and integral to building the kingdom of God.[14]

A hundred years later, during the Relief Society centennial year, the

First Presidency of the Church would declare, "We ask our Sisters of the Relief Society never to forget that they are a unique organization in the whole world, for they were organized under the inspiration of the Lord. . . . No other woman's organization in all the earth has had such a birth."[15]

Why Does What the Prophet Did and Said Matter?

As a young woman in my twenties, I had questions about where women fit in the Lord's Church. Then, in the early 1980s, while I was serving as the Relief Society president in that young adult ward, turmoil erupted in the United States surrounding the proposed Equal Rights Amendment, which proponents claimed would erase society's injustices toward women. Responding to revelation, Church leaders opposed the amendment. Sonia Johnson, a member of the Church, campaigned openly against the Church's position, and her advocacy made nationwide news.

Some of the women in my ward, most of whom had to support themselves, were confused about the Church's position. Others were downright upset. I struggled to understand the issue myself and then to know how to discuss it with women who wondered what could possibly be wrong with legislation that, on the surface, would pay them equally with men.

The spiritual struggle that ensued proved to be a vital learning experience for me. Ironically, it was during that era of upheaval about women in general that I came to feel complete peace with the roles our Father assigned His daughters. I began to grasp the breadth, distinctions, and magnificence of a righteous woman's influence—and that it comes from a divine endowment that has been in place from the beginning. Though women across the country were inflamed about equal rights, I became absolutely certain that in the only kingdom where it ultimately matters, our Father and His Son uphold women and regard us as central to the plan of salvation.

As Eliza R. Snow, second Relief Society general president, declared in those early days, "We want to be ladies in very deed, not according to the term of the word as the world judges, but fit companions of the Gods and Holy Ones. In an organized capacity we can assist each other in not only doing good but in refining ourselves, and whether few or many come forward and help to prosecute this great work, they will be those that will fill honorable positions in the Kingdom of God."[16]

Through the years, many personal experiences have magnified these truths.

I served as a stake Relief Society president under a stake president who mentored me both by what he said and by what he did. I had a standing invitation to bring anything to his attention that I felt he would want to know. Though I used his invitation sparingly, one day I raised a concern about an unproductive pattern I had observed in the working relationships some bishops had with their auxiliary presidents. He responded by inviting me to join him in addressing the subject at an upcoming bishops' training meeting. At the appointed hour, I arrived at the stake center and waited to be invited into the meeting.

When the door opened and I entered the high council room, the stake president quickly rose to his feet, and all the other men followed suit. This unexpected gesture of respect took my breath away, and a wave of emotion rushed over me. The stake president gestured toward the table where he and his counselors were sitting and said, "Sister Dew, please join us. We have a seat for you with us." He then introduced me by saying, "Brethren, I have invited Sister Dew to discuss a subject *we are both* concerned about. Please listen carefully to what she has to say."

I then delivered the message. When I concluded, the stake president said, "I endorse everything Sister Dew has taught and ask you to act on her suggestions."

Imagine how I felt about serving with a stake president who treated me as a trusted member of his team. I would have walked barefoot on hot coals to help him accomplish the Lord's objectives for our stake.

That experience was literally one of hundreds that demonstrated for me the powerful results of priesthood leaders and auxiliary leaders who unite in purpose and effort. Sister Julie B. Beck, former Relief Society general president, taught that "quorums and Relief Societies are an organized discipleship with the responsibility to assist in our Father's work to bring about eternal life for His children. We are not in the entertainment business; we are in the salvation business. . . . Where quorums and Relief Societies are unified in this work, they each essentially take an oar in the boat—each helping us move toward salvation."[17]

At all levels of Church government, I've had rewarding experiences with priesthood leaders. I have also had difficult and confusing experiences. But does a difficult experience with a priesthood leader mean that priesthood keys aren't real or that there is something inherently wrong with the way the Lord has organized His Church? Of course not. In a Church of fourteen-million-plus members, it is inevitable that some priesthood leaders (and some auxiliary leaders, for that matter) won't handle their authority or their assignments well. It's important to remember that leaders have differing degrees of experience and understanding. Years ago, Elder Marvin J. Ashton of the Quorum of the Twelve said to me, "Sheri, don't ever allow yourself to be offended by someone who is learning his job." That is wise counsel.

President Spencer W. Kimball admonished priesthood leaders that "our sisters do not wish to be indulged or to be treated condescendingly; they desire to be respected and revered as our sisters and our equals. I mention [this], my brethren, not because the doctrines or the teachings of the Church regarding women are in any doubt, but because in some situations our behavior is of doubtful quality."[18]

From my experience, most priesthood leaders earnestly seek the help of heaven as they strive to serve the Lord and the people for whom they have responsibility.

When all is said and done, every meaningful opportunity I've ever had to serve and progress has come to me *because* of my membership in the Church. Every single one. And *most* opportunities have been the direct result of a priesthood leader's influence. I have experienced for myself that what the Prophet demonstrated in his interactions with the women of Nauvoo reflects the reality that women hold a vital position in the Church and in the affections of the Lord.

Through the years, I have searched to find *any* organization *anywhere*—any business, charity, religion, or government—where *as many* women have *as much* responsibility and influence as in The Church of Jesus Christ of Latter-day Saints. I cannot find even one. Today millions of Latter-day Saint women in 170-plus countries teach, preach, pray, lead, and preside over auxiliary organizations. And it all began in Nauvoo in 1842 because a prophet of God organized the women according to the pattern of the Lord.

As an integral part of the Restoration, Joseph Smith restored woman to her rightful place.

THE PRIESTHOOD

What Did the Prophet Teach the Women about Priesthood, and Why?

Joseph Smith taught the women the order of heaven, beginning with the truth that priesthood keys, priesthood authority, and priesthood power were as relevant to them as they were to men.

In two of Joseph's sermons in particular, he taught about the blessings of the priesthood related to the temple. During his March 30 message, he declared that "the Society should move according to the ancient Priesthood," explaining that the women of Relief Society must become a "select Society separate from all the evils of the world, choice, virtuous and holy."[19]

The "ancient Priesthood" to which the Prophet referred is the higher or Melchizedek Priesthood, through which authority Church leaders "administer all the spiritual work of the Church."[20] This priesthood provides all of us—men and women—with access to God's greatest blessings. These include the supernal privileges of having the "heavens opened unto [us]" and "receiving the mysteries of the kingdom of heaven,"[21] which the Lord defined as "the key of the knowledge of God."[22] So when Joseph Smith instructed the women to "move according to the ancient Priesthood," he was not only indicating the power under which the Relief Society would operate but inviting the sisters to prepare for sacred temple ordinances, which ordinances would bless them with an endowment of knowledge and power that would open the heavens to them.

A month later, on April 28, in the most doctrinally significant of the six sermons, Joseph pursued this theme again, explaining that the purpose "of his being present on the occasion was, to make observations respecting the Priesthood."[23] The Prophet then delivered a message that can be confusing because he used the word *keys* in two ways: first, by referring to priesthood keys, which he exercised in behalf of the sisters; and second, by referring to the keys of knowledge, intelligence, and power that provide those who are endowed in the temple with access to God.

First, priesthood keys "are the authority God has given to priesthood leaders to direct, control, and govern the use of His priesthood on earth."[24] By definition, keys open things. Thus, those who hold priesthood keys open the flow of priesthood power in behalf of all who serve under their direction. They also have the right and authority to direct and govern the use of the priesthood within their jurisdiction.[25] When Joseph declared, "I now turn the key to you in the name of God and this Society shall rejoice and knowledge and intelligence shall flow down from this time—this is the beginning of better days, to this Society,"[26] he was exercising priesthood keys to authorize the flow of priesthood power in behalf of women and to formally open for them the privilege of serving, leading, and teaching in the Church.[27]

Elder Dallin H. Oaks taught that "when he 'turn[ed] the key,' the Prophet Joseph Smith made the Relief Society an official part of the Church and kingdom of God. This opened to women new opportunities for receiving knowledge and intelligence from on high, such as through the temple ordinances that were soon to be instituted. . . . No priesthood keys were delivered to the Relief Society. Keys are conferred on individuals, not organizations."[28] But because the Relief Society functions under the direction of those who hold priesthood keys, it has a power and authority to bless and strengthen the lives of women that no other organization for women can claim.

President George Albert Smith taught that when Joseph Smith "turned the key for the emancipation of womankind, it was turned for all the world, and from generation to generation the number of women who can enjoy the blessings of religious liberty and civil liberty has been increasing."[29] Nearly every major advancement benefitting women occurred *after* the Prophet used priesthood keys to open privileges for women.

The second way in which the Prophet used the word *keys* in his April 28 sermon referred to keys of knowledge, intelligence, and power obtained in the temple. Specifically, he spoke of "delivering the keys to this Society and to the church. . . . The keys of the kingdom are about to be given them, that they may be able to detect every thing false."[30]

Elder George A. Smith amplified this text in his account of this meeting in the *History of the Church:* "[Joseph] spoke of delivering the keys of the Priesthood to the Church, and said that the faithful members of the Relief Society should receive them in connection with their husbands, that the Saints whose integrity has been tried and proved faithful, might know how to ask the Lord and receive an answer."[31] In this usage, the Prophet was not referring to priesthood keys held by priesthood leaders, and he was not suggesting that Relief Society leaders would receive priesthood keys. He was, however, indicating that the "keys" that enable us to "detect everything false"—meaning the keys of knowledge, intelligence, and power given to the endowed—would be given women as well as men. These keys provide access to heaven—meaning access to godly power, to personal revelation, and to heavenly help.

In this context, Joseph's oft-quoted statement to the sisters has greater meaning than is perhaps commonly understood: "If you live up to your privileges, the angels cannot be restrain'd from being your associates—females, if they are pure and innocent can come into the presence of God."[32] In short, men and women who are endowed receive privileges in the temple that open up the heavens for those who learn how to do so.

The Prophet organized the women according to the pattern of the priesthood, taught them the doctrine of the priesthood, and organized them so that they were now included within the Church organization in a manner that mirrored the divine pattern of the celestial union of man and woman required for exaltation. He also taught that this pattern would soon be evident in the highest priesthood ordinances conferred in the temple. Bishop Newel K. Whitney told the sisters with the Prophet present that "without the female all things cannot be restor'd to the earth—it takes all to restore the Priesthood."[33]

Admittedly, there are additional statements in the April 28 sermon about women and priesthood that can be confusing. As an example, Joseph stated that "if the sisters should have faith to heal the sick, let all hold their tongues, and let every thing roll on"; and that there was no more sin in a "female laying hands on the sick than in wetting the face with water—that it is no sin for any body to do it that has faith." He also "offered instruction respecting the propriety of females administering to the sick by the laying on of hands—said it was according to revelation."[34]

The account of the latter statement in the *History of the Church* was amplified: "President Smith then gave instruction respecting the propriety of females administering to the sick by the prayer of faith, the laying on hands, or the anointing of oil; and said it was according to revelation that the sick should be nursed with herbs and mild food. . . . Who are better qualified to administer than our faithful and zealous sisters, whose hearts are full of faith, tenderness, sympathy and compassion. No one."[35]

What are we to make of the fact that these statements don't square with Church doctrine and practices today? The truth is that we don't know. Was the Prophet Joseph referring to prayers of faith and comfort rather than an exercise of priesthood power? Or was he anticipating the role women would play in the temple? Or had issues regarding women and priesthood not yet been fully revealed to him in the line-upon-line pattern of Restoration? Or were there reasons the Lord allowed women to give blessings of healing during those early, turbulent days when illness threatened many lives, priesthood bearers were frequently away, and women often found themselves alone? Or are there reasons above and beyond any of these? We don't know. The Lord's ways are not our ways. Our understanding is miniscule compared to His.

What we do know is that today priesthood blessings may be conferred only by those who have been ordained with priesthood authority, meaning only men. When all is said and done, this is a matter of faith—faith in Jesus Christ and the manner in which He has organized His Church, faith in the principle of continuing revelation, and faith that prophets, seers, and revelators who hold all the keys are exercising those keys as the Lord directs.[36]

Clearly, the lack of priesthood ordination does not preclude faithful women from having authority or access to power. President Joseph Fielding Smith taught that when Joseph Smith "turn[ed] the key" in behalf of women, he opened to them the privilege of exercising "some measure of divine authority, particularly in the direction of government and instruction in behalf of the women of the Church."[37] On another occasion President Smith stated, "While the sisters have not been given the Priesthood, . . . that does not mean that the Lord has not given unto them authority. Authority and Priesthood are two different things. A person may have authority given to him, or a sister to her, to do certain things in the Church that are binding and absolutely necessary for our salvation, such as the work that our sisters do in the House of the Lord."[38]

Further, President Gordon B. Hinckley taught women that prayers of faith would save the sick and that it was their "privilege to pray, with the full expectation that your Father in Heaven will hear that prayer when it is offered in faith."[39] And Elder Dallin H. Oaks explained that men and women alike may "pray directly to our Heavenly Father . . . by the channels He has established, without any mortal intermediary."[40]

And finally, President Boyd K. Packer articulated how vital the influence of women is in the Lord's kingdom when he taught that "however much priesthood power and authority the men may possess—however much wisdom and experience they may accumulate—the safety of the family, the integrity of the doctrine, the ordinances, the covenants, indeed the future of the Church, rests equally upon the women."[41]

When all is said and done, and regardless of changes that have occurred regarding women and priesthood since those early days, it is clear that the Prophet wanted women to understand not only that the doctrine of the priesthood was relevant to them but that they were the beneficiaries of its power and privileges.

Why Does What the Prophet Taught about Priesthood Matter?

For as long as I can remember, the exercise of priesthood power has moved me. Even as a young girl, I somehow just knew that priesthood power was real—that it really was the power and authority of God, and that we really could call upon it to bless, heal, protect, and strengthen us.

Perhaps for that reason, I've never been troubled about women not being ordained. But along the way, I have found myself serving women who *were* troubled and even burdened with the false notion that a lack of ordination for women is proof positive that women are not as valued as men by the Lord or at least by His Church. Because of this, there came a time when I realized that a testimony of the divinity of priesthood was not enough. I needed to understand the doctrine of the priesthood better so that I could help sisters who were confused. The Prophet's early sermons to women played a role in this. They didn't answer my questions about priesthood, but they did help me realize how important it was for me as a woman to understand my relationship to the priesthood. If Joseph wanted the women of Nauvoo to understand priesthood, then I wanted to understand it as well.

That desire sent me to the scriptures. I read passages on priesthood over and over again. Sections 20, 76, 84, 107, 121, and 124 of the Doctrine and Covenants for starters, along with Alma 13, became my friends. I wanted to understand what priesthood keys are, and what the distinction is between priesthood keys, priesthood authority, and priesthood power. In short, keys are the right to preside. Priesthood authority is conferred through ordination and is required to perform all sacred and saving ordinances.[42] And priesthood power is the power of God that emanates from the priesthood, which power is as available to women— particularly endowed women—as to men. I wanted to understand how to draw upon that power.

As women, we do ourselves an injustice if we assume that only men need to understand the priesthood. And we diminish God's power when we equate *holders of the priesthood* with *priesthood power*. Statements such as, "We would like to thank the priesthood for setting up the chairs," or

"I'm so grateful to have the priesthood in my home" are not accurate and do not do the priesthood justice. Priesthood is not synonymous with men. Priesthood *holders* are men. "The priesthood" refers to keys, authority, and power—God's power.

Elder Bruce R. McConkie taught that the "doctrine of the priesthood—unknown in the world and but little known even in the Church—cannot be learned out of the scriptures alone. . . . The doctrine of the priesthood is known only by personal revelation. It comes, line upon line and precept upon precept, by the power of the Holy Ghost to those who love and serve God with all their heart, might, mind, and strength."[43]

Joseph Smith was explicit on this point, telling the sisters that the signs or evidences of spiritual power, "such as healing the sick, casting out devils &c. should follow all that believe whether male or female."[44]

Though the priesthood cannot be fully understood through the scriptures alone, they are the place to begin. They teach that by virtue of the power and authority of the Melchizedek Priesthood, men and women alike may receive *all* of the ordinances of salvation, including baptism, receiving the Holy Ghost, the endowment, and sealing. They teach that the blessings of priesthood power—to be healed, to receive revelation, to speak and lead as directed by the Spirit, to receive the mysteries of the kingdom, to have the heavens opened, to enjoy the ministering of angels, and so on—are available equally to worthy, seeking men and women.[45] Gender is not, and has never been, a qualifier for receiving the blessings of priesthood power.

Said Elder Bruce R. McConkie, "Where spiritual things are concerned, as pertaining to all of the gifts of the Spirit, with reference to the receipt of revelation, the gaining of testimonies, and the seeing of visions, in all matters that pertain to godliness and holiness and which are brought to pass as a result of personal righteousness—in all these things men and women stand in a position of absolute equality before the Lord."[46] It is precisely because the Melchizedek Priesthood has been restored that these blessings are available to all.

The ultimate aim of the Melchizedek Priesthood is to enable men and women to be exalted. Exaltation is available *only* to a man and woman together, a couple who are sealed in the new and everlasting covenant of marriage,[47] who are true and faithful, and who qualify for a "fulness and a continuation of the seeds forever and ever."[48] No one will be exalted alone.

Elder John A. Widtsoe explained that "the Priesthood is for the benefit of all members of the Church. Men have no greater claim than women upon the blessings that issue from the Priesthood and accompany its possession. Woman does not hold the Priesthood, but she is a partaker of the blessings of the Priesthood. . . . This is made clear . . . in the Temple. . . . The ordinances of the Temple are distinctly of Priesthood character, yet women have access to *all* of them, and the highest blessings of the Temple are conferred only upon a man and his wife jointly."[49]

Why aren't women ordained to the priesthood here in mortality? We don't know. This is one of any number of things that the Lord has not yet elected to explain to us. But He has declared His will. Women are not assigned to direct the ecclesiastical affairs of the Church, nor are they required or eligible to be ordained, whereas men are. It is significant to note, however, that even worthy priesthood bearers are not able to perform saving ordinances without the approval of those with priesthood keys. For example, a Melchizedek Priesthood holder cannot baptize his daughter without the approval of his bishop or ordain his son an elder without the approval of his stake president. Even worthy men may exercise priesthood power only within boundaries the Lord has set.

On the other hand, women are not required to hold the priesthood to enter the house of the Lord, though the ordinances performed there are priesthood in nature, whereas men are. Neither are women required to hold the priesthood to serve as leaders in the Church. Further, the Lord has blessed His daughters with certain distinctive, divine gifts—including, said Joseph Smith, "feelings of charity,"[50] which result in an innate ability and desire to nurture and love. The gift of charity is the culminating gift of the Spirit, for it embodies almost all others. And women are blessed with a propensity for this gift.

I happily accept the Lord's pattern for the governance of His Church, knowing that it is inconsistent with the character of God for Him to love, cherish, or favor His sons more than His daughters, or His daughters more than His sons.

The keys to understanding priesthood keys, priesthood authority, and priesthood power reside in the temple, the scriptures, the teachings of prophets ancient and modern, and the whisperings of the Spirit. If you desire such a testimony, I invite you to study everything you can find from those sources about the priesthood. As you study, identify questions to ponder and pray about.

Some questions might include: If the Melchizedek Priesthood holds the "key of the mysteries of the kingdom, even the key of the knowledge of God," what does that mean?[51] If the Melchizedek Priesthood holds "the keys of all the spiritual blessings of the church," is that any different for men than it is for women?[52] How do the promises found in D&C 76 relate to the promises of D&C 107? With what were we endowed in the house of the Lord? What is a fulness of the priesthood?

Sincere questions lead the earnest seeker to knowledge and revelation.

Do I fully understand the doctrine of the priesthood? Of course not. I feel as though I am a doctrinal neophyte. I do know, however, that if we sincerely want to learn about the Lord and His ways, He will lead us along just as He did the Prophet Joseph, here a little and there a little. The Prophet himself taught us that.[53]

In that spirit, I share an example of being led along. One day, I became curious about a passage in D&C 84, which contains the oath and covenant of the priesthood. There we learn that those who are faithful and who "obtain" the Aaronic or Melchizedek Priesthood and then magnify their callings become "the sons of Moses and of Aaron and the seed of Abraham . . . and the elect of God."[54] These verses seem to apply specifically and solely to men.

Subsequent verses, however, say this: "And *also all they* who *receive* this priesthood *receive* me, saith the Lord; For he that *receiveth* my servants *receiveth* me; and he that *receiveth* me *receiveth* my Father; and he that *receiveth* my Father *receiveth* my Father's kingdom; therefore all that my Father hath shall be given unto him. And this is according to the oath and covenant which belongeth to the priesthood. Therefore, all those who *receive* the priesthood, *receive* this oath and covenant of my Father."[55]

The words *also all they* and the word *receive,* used no less than ten times in these verses, struck my curiosity. *Also all they* seem to imply more than those who are ordained. And though we typically use *receive* to mean "to acquire" something, the dictionary says that *receive* also means "to believe" or "to accept as true."

Interestingly, this secondary definition of *receive* is used frequently in the scriptures, often by the Lord Himself. For example, He began a revelation to Emma Smith by declaring that "all those who *receive* my gospel are sons and daughters in my kingdom."[56] When the Savior appeared to the Nephites, He lamented, "I came unto my own, and my own *received* [accepted, believed] me not. . . . And as many as have *received* me, to them have I given to become the sons of God."[57]

As I pondered the secondary definition of *receive,* I found myself wondering if the promises of D&C 84:35–40 might refer not only to those who receive the priesthood through ordination but also to those who receive it (meaning access to its blessings) by *believing* that the priesthood is the power of God, by *accepting* the manner in which the Lord has organized His kingdom, by sustaining those who hold priesthood keys, and by honoring priesthood power as the power of God. If so, is it possible that the blessings of the oath and covenant of the priesthood are efficacious in the lives of both men and women?

I do not share these ponderings as doctrine but as reflections of someone engaged in the step-by-step, line-upon-line process of learning and seeking. At the very least, it is clear from the scriptures that women have claim upon *all* blessings that emanate from priesthood keys, priesthood authority, and priesthood power.

I learned in an unforgettable way how real the power of priesthood keys is and how blessed we are by them. While I was serving in the Relief Society general presidency, another general officer and I traveled in a distant land with the Area President and his wife to a large city where the Church has many stakes—enough that one stake center could not accommodate all of the priesthood and auxiliary leaders assigned to attend the auxiliary training meetings in which we were participating. The Area President accompanied the other general officer to her meetings and asked me to go to a different chapel to teach the Relief Society and priesthood leaders assigned to that session. "Who will preside at the Relief Society training?" I asked. He responded that one of the stake presidents there had been assigned to preside, and off I went.

When I arrived at my building, I found a stake center filled to capacity and many stake presidents waiting to greet and help me; but due to a miscommunication, no one had received the assignment to preside from those who had keys. Because no stake president felt he could appoint himself to preside, no one did.

The meeting that unfolded has to be the worst meeting in the history of the dispensation. It was a disaster. From the moment I stood to teach a three-hour session, it was clear to me (and I'm sure to everyone else) that I was on my own. That night I experienced the utter futility of attempting to serve without the power of a presiding authority. *Priesthood keys are real.* They unlock the power of God to all who serve under their direction. *Priesthood power is real.* It is not some theological theory. It is the power of God Himself.

Joseph Smith taught that "the Melchizedek Priesthood . . . is the grand head, and . . . is the channel through which all knowledge, doctrine, the plan of salvation and every important matter is revealed from heaven."[58] What we understand and how we feel about the priesthood is central to our testimony of the restored gospel.

Though there are things about the priesthood as it relates to both men and women that I don't understand, this does not concern me, because wrestling with spiritual questions is a fundamental aspect of mortality. It is an exercise that strengthens our faith and spurs our growth, if we'll allow it to. Learning, after all, is integral to progression. Brigham Young explained that "we do not expect to cease learning while we live on earth; and when we pass through the veil, we expect still to continue to learn . . . [W]e are not capacitated to receive all knowledge at once. We must therefore receive a little here and a little there."[59]

In any case, the things I don't yet understand do not negate what I *do* know: that Joseph Smith was a prophet, foreordained by the Lord to restore His gospel, and that we have a living prophet today; that the priesthood has been restored to the earth; and that priesthood keys literally unlock God's power in behalf of all of us.

It may well be that some of the most defining tests of mortality are issues that swirl around gender, including how men feel about women; how women feel about men; how men feel about manhood and women about womanhood; and how all regard and honor priesthood keys, priesthood authority, and priesthood power.

When all is said and done, when Joseph Smith organized the Relief Society, he gave power to the work of women because women were now able to work through priesthood keys. And *that* is what distinguishes the Relief Society from any other women's organization in the world.

THE TEMPLE

What Did the Prophet Teach about the Temple?

Many of the Prophet's teachings about priesthood also have bearing in a discussion about the temple because priesthood and temple are inseparable. So please think of the teachings on the temple as an extension of the teachings about the priesthood.

It was interest in supporting the work of building the temple that led to the founding of Relief Society in the first place. But the link between Relief Society and the temple goes far beyond that.

In early 1842, with the Nauvoo Temple in progress, Joseph wrote that its completion would be "an event of the greatest importance to the

Church and the world, making the Saints in Zion to rejoice, and the hypocrite and sinner to tremble." He added that all things were coming together to bring about "the completion of the fullness of the Gospel, a fullness of the dispensation of dispensations, even the fullness of times."[60]

He had, after all, received many revelations through the years about the temple. And then just three months before he was martyred, he made this defining statement: "We need the temple more than anything else."[61] Indeed, the Prophet told the sisters that "the church is not now organiz'd in its proper order, and cannot be until the Temple is completed."[62]

Some believed that a major reason the Relief Society was organized was to prepare the sisters for the temple. Reynolds Cahoon, a member of the Nauvoo Temple building committee, told the sisters that "this Society is raisd by the Lord to prepare us for the great blessings which are for us in the House of the Lord."[63]

As Joseph taught the sisters, the temple was clearly on his mind. He implored them to be pure, to act in holiness, and to resist evil. "Meekness, love, purity, these are the things that should magnify us," he declared, promising, "If you will be pure, nothing can hinder."[64] The purpose of the Relief Society was to help the sisters "practice holiness," he declared.[65]

All of his teachings were designed to help the sisters be worthy of the "keys of the kingdom," meaning keys of knowledge and intelligence found in the temple that provide greater access to heaven. His promise was clear, that "the keys of the kingdom are about to be given to them, that they may be able to detect every thing false."[66]

Bishop Newel K. Whitney had already received his endowment

when he told the sisters in a Relief Society meeting: "God has many precious things to bestow, even to our astonishment if we are faithful. . . . I rejoice that God has given us means whereby we may get intelligence and instruction." He then encouraged them to prepare to receive "grace for grace, light and intelligence—if we have intelligence we have pow'r— knowledge is power."[67]

The Minutes demonstrate that before Joseph ever gave the endowment ordinances in their fulness (on May 4, 1842), he intended for women to receive ordinances promising them that they would be queens and priestesses in eternity. He also taught that husbands and wives would together receive the fulness of priesthood blessings.[68]

Elder James E. Talmage would later explain: "The Holy Priesthood is conferred, as an individual bestowal, upon men only, and this in accordance with Divine requirement. It is not given to woman to exercise the authority of the Priesthood independently; nevertheless, in the sacred endowments associated with the ordinances pertaining to the House of the Lord, woman shares with man the blessings of the Priesthood. When the frailties and imperfections of mortality are left behind . . . husband and wife will administer in their respective stations, seeing and understanding alike, and co-operating to the full in the government of their family kingdom. Then shall woman be recompensed in rich measure for all the injustice that womanhood has endured in mortality. . . . Mortal eye cannot see nor mind comprehend the beauty, glory, and majesty of a righteous woman made perfect in the celestial kingdom of God."[69]

Six days after the Prophet's landmark sermon of April 28, in which he promised the sisters that those "whose integrity has been tried and proved faithful, might know how to ask the Lord and receive an answer,"[70] Joseph performed the first endowments in this dispensation in the upper room of the red brick store.[71]

In doing so, he made it possible for those who become sons and daughters of Christ to receive the fulness of the blessings the Father has for His children, explaining that "there was nothing made known to these men but what will be made known to all the Saints of the last days, so soon as they are prepared to receive [them]."[72]

It would be more than a year before the first woman, Emma Smith, received the endowment (on September 23, 1843), but some three thousand women would follow suit before the expulsion from Nauvoo, blessing them with covenant-making protection and power. Many would experience what Joseph promised one sister—that the endowment "will bring you out of darkness into marvelous light."[73]

Elizabeth Ann Whitney, who was one of thirty-six women called to serve as Nauvoo Temple ordinance workers, later recalled, "I gave myself, my time and attention to that mission. I worked in the Temple every day without cessation until it was closed."[74]

After the Nauvoo Temple was dedicated, the Saints were so eager to receive their ordinances that Brigham Young recorded: "I have given myself up entirely to the work of the Lord in the Temple night and day, not taking more than four hours sleep, upon average, per day, and going home but once a week."[75]

Sarah Rich, who also worked in the Nauvoo Temple, later

explained the impact of the temple on those who endured the trek west: "If it had not been for the faith and knowledge that was bestowed upon us in that temple . . . , our journey would have been like one taking a leap in the dark. To start out . . . in the winter as it were and in our state of poverty, it would seem like walking into the jaws of death. But we had faith in our Heavenly Father, and we put our trust in Him feeling that we were His chosen people . . . , and instead of sorrow, we felt to rejoice that the day of our deliverance had come."[76]

It is significant that many sisters received the highest ordinances of the priesthood *prior* to heading west. The Prophet Joseph's 1842 sermons were designed to prepare the sisters to make and keep sacred covenants that would bind them to the Lord—covenants that would endow them with power, intelligence, and knowledge. Joseph was the only man on earth who could prepare them to face what lay ahead.

Does the Prophet's Emphasis on the Temple Have Significance for Us?

The nature of our challenges differs from that of our sisters of yesteryear. Though we may not have to pull handcarts through the dead of winter, we all climb our own Rocky Ridge at some time—or more likely, many times—during this journey in the wilderness called mortality. The causes of steep climbs vary: loneliness and betrayal, loss and prolonged disappointment, wavering testimonies and splintered families. There are enough Rocky Ridges to go around. Through it all, the temple is an incomparable lifeline because the temple is filled with knowledge and spiritual power.

President Howard W. Hunter pleaded with us to "look to the temple of the Lord as the great symbol of [our] membership."[77] The importance of that statement cannot be overemphasized. Baptism opens the gate to the celestial kingdom, but the temple opens the gate to exaltation.[78]

President Thomas S. Monson promised that "as you and I go to the holy houses of God, . . . we will be more able to bear *every* trial and to overcome *each* temptation."[79]

While presiding over the Bountiful Utah Temple, President Douglas L. Callister told a group of young adults that "when we enter the temple, we leave the world of make-believe."[80] Indeed, the artificial, unseemly, confusing elements of mortal life fade away as we enter the temple to worship, learn, and communicate with the heavens.

My own Rocky Ridges would have crushed me long ago if I had not discovered that the temple is a place of refuge, a place of knowledge, a place of peace and power, and a place where we learn how close heaven and those who reside there actually are. But it didn't begin that way for me.

I was in my late twenties when I received my endowment, and frankly, the temple intimidated me at first. One day a couple of years later, my stake president asked me simply, "How often do you go to the temple?"

After an awkward pause, I admitted, "Not as often as I should."

The way he responded was perfect for me: "You might want to think about that."

That was all it took. I walked out of his office knowing that his question and response had been a gentle but heaven-sent rebuke. I had allowed my apprehensions to shortchange not only the Lord but my spiritual growth.

I began to attend the temple regularly—at first out of sheer obedience. But before long, my experience in the temple began to change. I began to listen and pray differently, to have more meaningful thoughts and impressions, and to ask different, and better, questions. Little by little, I began to have flashes of learning and moments of revelation.

I'll never forget the day when I realized that going to the temple was no longer a "have-to." I *wanted* to be there. I *needed* to be there, and as often as I could. The temple helped me feel safer, stronger, and more at peace. Some of the clearest answers I've received to life's thorny challenges have come in the temple. And many insights about the gospel have come while I have been worshiping there. It is a house of truth filled with spiritual power. In the temple, we learn how to learn about the things of God.

For all the many times I've been to the temple, the depth and breadth of all the Lord has for us in His house—the covenants, privileges, promises, knowledge, and power—far exceed what my puny mind at present comprehends. But going there regularly puts me in the best possible position to grow, learn, and step completely outside the world into a place where I can be reminded about things as they really are and really will be.

The temple isn't supposed to be easy to understand. It is a step-by-step ascent toward God—and there's nothing simplistic about that. Elder John A. Widtsoe wrote that "the endowment is so richly symbolic that only a fool would attempt to describe it; it is so packed full of revelations to those who exercise their strength to seek and see, that no human words can explain or make clear the possibilities that reside in the temple service. The endowment which was given by revelation can best be understood by revelation."[81]

Gaining spiritual knowledge takes work. Joseph Smith wrote from Liberty Jail: "The things of God are of deep import; and time, and experience, and careful and ponderous and solemn thoughts can only find them out. Thy mind, O man! if thou wilt lead a soul unto salvation, must stretch as high as the utmost heavens, and search into and contemplate the darkest abyss, and the broad expanse of eternity—thou must commune with God."[82]

Scriptures on the temple (there are more than three hundred in the Doctrine and Covenants alone) help unlock revelation as well as *how to receive* revelation. The Lord told Joseph that He would endow those whom He had chosen with "power from on high."[83] Christ is the source of that power. The temple is His—which is why it contains keys that unlock the wonders of eternity, the mysteries of the kingdom, and the power of God.

In D&C 109 alone, we are promised that all who enter the Lord's house will feel His power; that they will receive a fulness of the Holy Ghost and emerge from the temple armed with power; that they will have the Lord's glory around them and angels to take charge over them; that they will receive a testimony of the covenant and not faint in days of trouble.[84]

These verses, along with many others, prompt numerous questions that can guide our temple worship and lead to revelation: What is a fulness of the Holy Ghost, and how does one receive it? What did the Lord mean when He said we leave the temple armed with power? What do we learn in the temple about prayer, about dealing with the adversary, and about parting the veil? How does the Lord's glory manifest itself in our lives? What does it mean to have a testimony of the covenant? How does the temple help us understand who we are? And many more.

It has been said that in the next life, there will be only one sorrow: not to be a Saint. The temple is the only place on earth where we may receive the highest ordinances and greatest spiritual privileges and powers of mortality. It is the ultimate institution of higher learning. The best education in the world pales compared to what the Grand Schoolmaster will teach us if we are willing to submit to His curriculum taught in His House.

I served as a guide during VIP week of the Manhattan Temple open house; in preparation, a General Authority counseled us about how to conduct the tours. "Less is more," he said. "When it comes to guiding people through the temple, the Lord likes to do His own teaching in His own house."

And so He does.

CHARITY AND THE DIVINE NATURE OF WOMEN

What Did the Prophet Teach Women about Their Divine Nature?

Joseph taught the sisters that inherent within their natures were spiritual gifts, beginning with the gift of charity.

Joseph was the embodiment of charity. Even as he suffered the hideous incarceration in the Liberty Jail, he admonished his people, "Let thy bowels also be full of charity towards all men, and to the household of faith," promising that if they did, the "doctrine of the priesthood" would distil upon their souls as the dews from heaven.[85]

The Prophet understood that women have a remarkable capacity to understand things of the Spirit and of the heart. As he taught them about their divinely endowed strengths, he added awe-inspiring promises: "The charitable Society—this is according to your natures—it is natural for females to have feelings of charity—you are now plac'd in a situation where you can act according to those sympathies which God has planted in your bosoms. . . .—if you live up to your privileges, the angels cannot be restrain'd from being your associates—females, if they are pure and innocent can come into the presence of God."[86]

This one statement alone is laden with both doctrine and promise: that our Father endowed His daughters with charity; that if we live up to the spiritual privileges of being a woman, angels can't be restrained from watching over and accompanying us;[87] and that purity will lead us into the presence of God.

⁕ In a later meeting, Joseph picked up the theme of charity again, explaining its power: "Nothing is so much calculated to lead people to forsake sin as to take them by the hand and watch over them with tenderness. When persons manifest the least kindness and love to me, O what pow'r it has over my mind, while the opposite course has a tendency to harrow up all the harsh feelings and depress the human mind." He continued with a warning and a promise: "'tis the doctrine of the devil to retard the human mind and retard our progress, by filling us with self-righteousness—The nearer we get to our heavenly Father, the more are we dispos'd to look with compassion on perishing souls—to take them upon our shoulders and cast their sins behind our back."[88]

No wonder he explained from the beginning that the purpose of Relief Society was to "save souls."[89]

Joseph Smith championed women and womanhood.

But he also cautioned women about their innate weaknesses and unrighteous tendencies, including behaviors that threaten charity. In fact, in *every single sermon* to the sisters of Nauvoo, he warned them about their tendency to gossip, backbite, and judge one another, and he took square aim at self-righteousness.

Acknowledging difficulties he had faced because of aspiring men, "great big Elders," as he called them, "who had caused him much trouble" and who had even proclaimed *his* revelations as their own, he warned the women that the "same aspiring disposition will be in this Society, and must be guarded against."[90] Here is just one warning from each sermon:

- "Do not injure the character of any one—if members of the Society shall conduct improperly, deal with them, and keep all your doings within your own bosoms, and hold all characters sacred."[91]
- "All must act in concert or nothing can be done."[92]
- "Don't be limited in your views with regard to your neighbors' virtues, but be limited towards your own virtues, and

not think yourselves more righteous than others; you must enlarge your souls toward others if [you would] do like Jesus."[93]

- "Put a double watch over the tongue. . . . The tongue is an unruly member—hold your tongues about things of no moment, a little tale will set the world on fire."[94]

- "We are full of selfishness—the devil flatters us that we are very righteous, while we are feeding on the faults of others."[95]

- "Little evils do the most injury to the church. If you have evil feelings and speak of them to one another, it has a tendency to do mischief."[96]

In cautioning the sisters about their weaknesses, the Prophet was also preparing them for the difficult days ahead, in which unity would be crucial. "By union of feeling we obtain pow'r with God," he taught the sisters.[97]

His words no doubt helped many. Helen Mar Whitney described the power of charity in operation during the exodus from Nauvoo: "The love of God flowed from heart to heart till the wicked one seemed powerless in his efforts to get between us and the Lord, and his cruel darts, in some instances, were shorn of their sting."[98]

What Is the Significance of What the Prophet Taught?

Bad girls. Mean girls. Selfish girls. Almost anywhere you look today, there are evidences—and plenty of them—of womanhood gone awry. The Apostle Paul warned that it would come to this. Foreseeing the last days, he described "silly women laden with sins, led away with divers lusts," who would be "ever learning, and never able to come to the knowledge of the truth."[99] And Isaiah foresaw "daughters of Zion" who had become "haughty."[100]

Let's face it: Today silly women mired in the sophistries and seductions of the world, and haughty women obsessed with themselves, abound. Regrettably, many women succumb to the temptation to judge, gossip, and undermine one another.

This is nothing if not predictable. Satan will do anything in his considerable power to neutralize the best of our divine nature by exploiting our vulnerabilities. He is expert at turning empathy into envy and charity into criticism. He knows that women filled with pride or jealousy are roadblocks to the Lord's work, and if he can preoccupy us with feelings of inferiority or superiority—he can exploit either—he has a natural inroad to afflict families, friendships, and communities.

And yet, of all women we ought to be women of charity.

We perhaps underestimate the significance of Joseph's statement that "it is natural for females to have feelings of charity," which are sympathies that "God has planted in [our] bosoms."[101]

Charity is not an emotion or an action. It is not something we feel or do. *Charity is who the Savior is.* It is His most defining and dominant attribute. It is what enabled Him to endure the Garden and the cross for you and me. It is one of the things that makes Him God. Thus, when we plead for the gift of charity, we aren't asking for kind feelings toward someone who has wounded us. We are pleading for our very natures to be changed, for our character to become more and more like the Savior's, so that we literally feel as He would feel and do what He would do. This is why Mormon said that when the Savior appears, those who have been gifted with charity will be like him, for they will "see him as he is."[102]

The one sure measure of an individual's conversion to Jesus Christ is how that person treats others—in other words, his or her charity. When we turn our hearts to the Lord, and as we increasingly become more like Him, we instinctively open our hearts to others. As one example of many, after Alma the Younger's conversion, his thoughts turned immediately to his people, for he "could not bear that any human soul should perish."[103]

Almost every major scriptural sermon—the Sermon on the Mount, King Benjamin's address, Alma's address at the Waters of Mormon, and a number of others—focuses on the way we treat each other. We are admonished to turn the other cheek, to be reconciled to each other, and to love our enemies and pray for those who despitefully use us.

And yet, we often fall for traps Lucifer has laid to estrange us from one another: gossiping, begrudging each others' successes, and judging one another.

I've lost count of the individuals who've asked if I feel guilty for "choosing a career over marriage." Those who ask that question remind me of speakers at an LDS-oriented symposium who took as their text several addresses I had given through the years. Unfortunately, those presenters spent more time misjudging my motives than evaluating what I had actually said. I was fascinated to learn that speakers whom I'd never met had announced that I'd *chosen* to remain single. There was no way they could have known—especially without asking me—about my years of intense spiritual work pleading for the blessing of marriage that seems to come so easily to so many. Why do some feel the need to judge?

But how often have you and I made judgments that are equally unfair? The Prophet Joseph's language was unmistakable: "Sisters of this Society, shall there be strife among you? I will not have it—you must repent and get the love of God. Away with selfrighteousness."[104]

It is simply not for us to judge each other. The Lord has reserved that right for Himself. Only He knows our hearts and understands the varying circumstances of our lives.

If there is anywhere in this world where a woman should feel that she belongs, it is in this Church and it is in the Relief Society. True charity never fails because the love of the Savior manifest through us won't fail. President Gordon B. Hinckley both challenged and promised us when he said: "Do you want to be happy? . . . Work to lift and serve His sons and daughters. You will come to know a happiness that you have never known before. . . Let's get the cankering, selfish attitude out of our lives . . . and stand a little taller . . . in the service of others."[105] And in a theme representative of his life, President Thomas S. Monson has counseled us to look beyond ourselves. "Unless we lose ourselves in service to others, there is little purpose to our own lives," he said. "Those who live only for themselves eventually shrivel up and figuratively lose their lives, while those who lose themselves in service to others grow and flourish—and in effect save their lives."[106]

I have seen charity in action in countless settings and cultures. One experience is a reflection of many others. I was called to serve in a stake Relief Society presidency at age thirty-two, and our presidency bonded quickly as dear friends. Because of my work schedule and their large families, we held presidency meetings on weekdays at 5:30 A.M.

One morning the president raised an issue that for some reason set me off. I climbed on my own Rameumptom, delivered a speech, and left in a huff. But as I drove away, my heart sank. I couldn't believe I had responded to friends in that way, was desperate to apologize, and counted the hours until I could do so.

Finally evening came. Intent on stopping at each of their homes to apologize, I ran by my house first, only to have the doorbell ring as soon as I walked in the door. There stood my friends, dinner in hand. I'll never forget what they said: "This morning wasn't like you. You must be under a lot of pressure. We thought dinner might make you feel better." I couldn't believe the pureness of their hearts. I cried as I apologized.

Imagine what they could have been saying all day. "That little brat!" They could have whipped themselves into a lather and punished me for days. But they didn't. Instead, they gave me the benefit of the doubt. That day I felt what charity feels like. Charity was not the casserole. It was the gentle way my friends handled my mistake. They reached out with compassion on a perishing soul.

Like our Nauvoo sisters who faced the trek west, we have lives that aren't likely to get any easier. We need each other's strength and compassion. We need to be able to lean on, learn from, and help each other along the path.

President Henry B. Eyring has frequently spoken about the virtue of unity. "You have heard [the] message of unity from me more than once," he acknowledged. "I may well speak of it in the future. I have heard it from every prophet of God in my lifetime. A plea for unity was the last message I remember from President David O. McKay. The Lord's prophets have always called for unity. The need for that gift to be granted to us and the challenge to maintain it will grow greater in the days ahead, in which we will be prepared as a people for our glorious destiny."[107]

Unity is a natural outgrowth of charity. If we live up to our privileges, including the privilege of being women blessed with spiritual gifts from our Father, we need never feel alone—because we'll have angels in heaven and on earth to walk beside us.

How Can Joseph's Sermons to the Sisters of This Dispensation Help Us?

I end where I began, with questions: Why would Joseph Smith have wanted the women of his day to understand the priesthood, the temple, their divine nature, and their standing in the Church? And does what he said to a small group of Latter-day Saint women 170 years ago matter now?

They have never mattered more. If we understand who we are, what God needs us to do, that we have access to the blessings of priesthood power, and that the temple is filled with that power, we place ourselves in an optimum position to fulfill the mission for which we were sent into mortality.

President Gordon B. Hinckley declared that when our Father

created woman, it was "the crowning of His glorious work." Said he, "I like to regard Eve as His masterpiece after all that had gone before."[108]

As modern-day daughters of Eve, as inheritors of her majesty and her potential, we have work to do and influence to wield.

Precisely because of our unprecedented access to both knowledge and technology, we can help advance the cause of Jesus Christ more than any women have ever been able to help. By the same token, however, we are equally well positioned to frustrate the cause of Christ.

Case in point: We have been encouraged to use technology to reach out, and LDS women have taken to the blogosphere in large numbers. Many blogs are excellent—articulate, engaging, inspiring, and right on point doctrinally. Some, however, are filled with a kind of "social gospel" that doesn't always represent either the Church or Latter-day Saint women very well. Most likely these writers don't mean any harm; they just don't know what we believe. And so their writings are composed of that unfortunate mixture of the philosophies of women sprinkled lightly with truth. The risk is not just in misrepresenting the Lord's Church but in selling it short.

Reflecting on his time with Joseph Smith, President Heber C. Kimball said that the greatest torment the Prophet Joseph endured "and the greatest mental suffering was because this people would not live up to their privileges. . . . He said sometimes that he felt . . . as though he were pent up in an acorn shell, and all because the people . . . would not prepare themselves to receive the rich treasures of wisdom and knowledge that he had to impart. He could have revealed a great many things to us if we had been ready; but he said there were many things that we could not receive because we lacked that diligence . . . necessary to entitle us to those choice things of the kingdom."[109]

In a similar lament, Nephi wrote that too many would "not search knowledge, nor understand great knowledge, when it is given unto them in plainness, even as plain as word can be."[110]

Joseph Smith's six sermons to women are as plain as word can be. I invite you to study them. Cross-reference his teachings with those of living prophets, seers, and revelators. Record your questions and learnings. What expands your understanding? What gives you hope? What prompts you to repent? What evokes charity? What gives you confidence to share what you believe with those not of our faith? Most important, what increases your faith in the Lord Jesus Christ?

Knowing more enables us to do more and to do better.

By the very nature of what he chose to teach women, Joseph Smith established expectations for every woman who would have the privilege of living in this great, culminating dispensation—the one foreseen by prophets since the beginning of time, the dispensation of the fulness of times. *Our* dispensation. And the first expectation is that we learn how to *receive* the truths, the spiritual gifts, and the privileges the Lord has offered His true followers.

Our sisters of Nauvoo helped lay the foundation of a great work. They did it against every kind of prevailing emotional, spiritual, and tangible wind.

Now it is our turn.

It is our chance on the big stage to help bear off the kingdom triumphantly. It wasn't easy for them, and it won't be easy for us.

But they did it, and so can we.

President Boyd K. Packer's unqualified endorsement of Relief Society is also an unqualified endorsement of the influence of the women of the Church: "I endorse the Relief Society without hesitation, for I know it to have been organized by inspiration from Almighty God. It has been blessed since its organization. I know that it is a rising, and not a setting, sun. I know that the light and the power that emanates from it will increase, not decrease."[111]

If we are willing to become the women the Prophet Joseph admonished us to become, women who are true followers of Jesus Christ, the encroaching darkness in the world will actually provide our opportunity. For the women of the world will look to us in increasing numbers and will see in the gospel a better way.

One woman who endured the trek west recorded afterward, "I am grateful I was counted worthy to be a pioneer." I am grateful you and I were counted worthy to come now, when everything is on the line, to be the women privileged to help prepare the world for the return of the Son of God.

We can do it. I know we can.

Notes

1. D&C 135:3.

2. In *Journal of Discourses*, 26 vols. (London: Latter-day Saints' Book Depot, 1856–1886), 23:362. A lengthier version of President Cannon's remarks reads: "He was visited constantly by angels; and the Son of God Himself condescended to come and minister unto him, the Father

having also shown Himself unto him; and these various angels, the heads of dispensations, having also ministered unto him. . . . [H]e had vision after vision in order that his mind might be fully saturated with a knowledge of the things of God, and that he might comprehend the great and holy calling that God has bestowed upon him. In this respect he stands unique. There is no man in this dispensation can occupy the station that he, Joseph did, God having reserved him and ordained him for that position, and bestowed upon him the necessary power."

3. Joseph Smith Jr., *History of the Church of Jesus Christ of Latter-day Saints,* 7 vols. (Salt Lake City: The Church of Jesus Christ of Latter-day Saints, 1932–1951), 6:50.

4. *History of the Church,* 5:402.

5. In Conference Report, April 1906, 3–4. On another occasion, President Joseph F. Smith said of Relief Society: "This organization is divinely made, divinely authorized, divinely instituted, divinely ordained of God to minister for the salvation of the souls of women and of men. Therefore there is not any organization that can compare with it, . . . that can ever occupy the same stand and platform that this can. . . . Make [Relief Society] first, make it foremost, make it the highest, the best and the deepest of any organization in existence in the world. You are called by the voice of the Prophet of God to do it, to be uppermost, to be the greatest and the best, the purest and the most devoted to the right" (*Teachings of Presidents of the Church: Joseph F. Smith* [Salt Lake City: The Church of Jesus Christ of Latter-day Saints, 1998], 184).

6. D&C 109:7.

7. Recorded by Sarah M. Kimball in 1882 in her capacity as general secretary of the Relief Society, as quoted in *Daughters in My Kingdom* (Salt Lake City: The Church of Jesus Christ of Latter-day Saints, 2011), 12.

8. *Nauvoo Relief Society Minute Book* (hereafter *Minutes*), March 17, 1842. Available online at http://josephsmithpapers.org/paperDetails/nauvoo-relief-society-minute-book?dm=image -and-text&zm=zoom-inner&tm=expanded&p=1&s=&sm=none.

9. Sarah M. Kimball, "Auto-biography," *Woman's Exponent,* September 1, 1883, 51. On another occasion, Sarah Kimball recalled the words differently, indicating that Joseph said, "I have desired to organize the Sisters in the order of the Priesthood. I now have the key by which I can do it. The organization of the Church of Christ was never perfect until the women were organized." Recorded by Sarah M. Kimball in 1882 in her capacity as general secretary of the Relief Society, "Relief Society Record, 1880–1892," 29, 30, Church History Library, Historical Department of The Church of Jesus Christ of Latter-day Saints.

10. D&C 27:6; 86:10; 109:23.

11. Many revelations and changes in Church administration and organization illustrate this, including the June 8, 1978, revelation extending the privilege of priesthood ordination to all worthy males, and the relatively recent addition of Churchwide Seventies Quorums.

12. After giving the first endowments, the Prophet turned to Brigham Young and said,

"Brother Brigham, this is not arranged perfectly; however we have done the best we could under the circumstances in which we are placed. I wish you to take this matter in hand: organize and systematize all these ceremonies" (L. John Nuttall diary, February 7, 1877; see also *BYU Studies* 19, Winter 1979, 159fn).

13. James E. Talmage, *Jesus the Christ* (Salt Lake City, Deseret Book, 1982), 442.

14. Women have always played central roles in the Savior's Church. About the Relief Society, Eliza R. Snow wrote that "although the name may be of modern date, the institution is of ancient origin. We were told by our martyred prophet that the same organization existed in the Church anciently" ("Female Relief Society," *Deseret News,* April 22, 1868).

15. First Presidency message, July 3, 1942, "To the Presidency, Officers and Members of the Relief Society," in *A Centenary of Relief Society, 1842–1942* (Salt Lake City: Deseret News Press, 1942), 7.

16. Eliza R. Snow, Address to Lehi Ward Relief Society, October 27, 1869, in *Relief Society Minute Book,* 1868–79, Church History Library, 26-27.

17. Julie B. Beck, "Why Are We Organized into Quorums and Relief Societies?" Brigham Young University Devotional address, January 17, 2012.

18. Spencer W. Kimball, "Our Sisters in the Church," *Ensign,* November 1979, 49.

19. *Minutes,* March 30, 1842.

20. *Handbook 2, Administering the Church* (Salt Lake City: The Church of Jesus Christ of Latter-day Saints, 2010), 8.

21. D&C 107:19.

22. D&C 84:19.

23. *Minutes,* April 28, 1842. Joseph Smith later described this address in these terms: "At two o'clock I met the members of the 'Female Relief Society,' and . . . gave a lecture on the Priesthood, showing how the sisters would come in possession of the privileges, blessings and gifts of the Priesthood, and that the signs should follow them, such as healing the sick, casting out devils, &c. and that they might attain unto these blessings by a virtuous life, and conversation, and diligence in keeping all the commandments" (*History of the Church,* 4:602).

24. *Handbook 2, Administering the Church,* 8. The handbook adds: "Those who hold priesthood keys have the right to preside over and direct the Church within a jurisdiction. Jesus Christ holds all the keys of the priesthood pertaining to His Church. He has conferred upon each of His Apostles all the keys that pertain to the kingdom of God on earth. The senior living Apostle, the President of the Church, is the only person on earth authorized to exercise all priesthood keys (see D&C 43:1–4; 81:2; 107: 64–67, 91–92; 132:7)."

25. *Handbook 2, Administering the Church* (page 8) explains how those other than the First Presidency and Quorum of the Twelve receive priesthood keys: "Seventies act by assignment and by the delegation of authority from the First Presidency and Quorum of the Twelve Apostles.

Area Presidents are assigned to administer areas under the authorization of the First Presidency and the Twelve. The Presidency of the Seventy are set apart and are given the keys to preside over the Quorums of Seventy.

"The President of the Church delegates priesthood keys to other priesthood leaders so they can preside in their areas of responsibility. Priesthood keys are bestowed on presidents of temples, missions, stakes, and districts; bishops; branch presidents; and quorum presidents. This presiding authority is valid only for the designated responsibilities and within the geographic jurisdiction of each leader's calling."

26. *Minutes,* April 28, 1842.

27. See Jill Mulvay Derr, Janath Russell Cannon, and Maureen Ursenbach Beecher, *Women of Covenant: The Story of Relief Society* (Salt Lake City: Deseret Book, 1992), 47–48 for further discussion on this point.

28. Dallin H. Oaks, "The Relief Society and the Church," *Ensign,* May 1992, 35–36. Elder Oaks further explained that "the same is true of priesthood authority and of the related authority exercised under priesthood direction. Organizations may channel the exercise of such authority, but they do not embody it. Thus, the priesthood keys were delivered to the members of the First Presidency and the Quorum of Twelve Apostles, not to any organizations."

29. George Albert Smith, "Address to Members of Relief Society," *Relief Society Magazine,* December 1945, 717. In that same address, President Smith told the sisters of Relief Society: "You are . . . more blessed than any other women in all the world. You were the first women to have the franchise; the first women to have a voice in the work of a church. It was God that gave it to you and it came as a result of revelation to a Prophet of the Lord."

30. *Minutes,* April 28, 1842.

31. *History of the Church,* 4:604.

32. *Minutes,* April 28, 1842. Bathsheba Smith, the fourth general president of the Relief Society, wrote that in a general fast meeting, Joseph "said that we did not know how to pray to have our prayers answered. But when I and my husband had our endowments. . . . Joseph Smith presiding, he taught us the order of prayer" (*Juvenile Instructor,* June 1, 1892, 27:345).

33. *Minutes,* May 27, 1842. Elder Dallin H. Oaks shared insight on this point as it relates to Relief Society: "One of the great functions of Relief Society is to provide sisterhood for women, just as priesthood quorums provide brotherhood for men. But all should remember that neither sisterhood nor brotherhood is an end in itself. . . . The ultimate and highest expression of womanhood and manhood is in the new and everlasting covenant of marriage between a man and a woman. Only this relationship culminates in exaltation" ("The Relief Society and the Church," *Ensign,* May 1992, 37).

34. *Minutes,* April 28, 1842.

35. *History of the Church,* 4:607. A second example of potential confusion about women

and priesthood centers around Eliza's recording that Joseph proposed to "ordain" the new Relief Society presidency to preside over the Society. Elder John Taylor later clarified that Emma did not receive priesthood keys or authority: "On the occasion of the organization of the Relief Society, by the Prophet Joseph Smith at Nauvoo, I was present Sister Emma Smith was elected president and Sisters Elizabeth Ann Whitney and Sarah M. Cleveland her Counselors. The Prophet Joseph then said that Sister Emma was named in the revelation recorded in the Book of Doctrine and Covenants concerning the Elect Lady, and furthermore that she had been ordained to expound the Scriptures. . . . The ordination then given did not mean the conferring of the Priesthood upon those sisters yet the sisters hold a portion of the Priesthood in coneciton with their husbands. (Sisters Eliza R. Snow and Bathsheba W. Smith, stated that they so understood it in Nauvoo and have looked upon it always in that light.) As I stated, at that meeting, I was called upon by the Prophet Joseph and I did then ordain Sisters Whitney and Cleveland, and blessed Sister Emma and set her apart. I could not ordain these sisters to anything more or to greater powers than had been conferred upon Sister Emma who had previously been ordained to expound the Scriptures, and that Joseph said at that time, that being an elect lady had its significance, and that the revelation was then fulfilled in Sister Emma being thus elected to preside over the Relief Society" (*Woman's Exponent,* September 1, 1880, 53).

36. Brigham Young taught: "It is the privilege of a mother to have faith and to administer to her child; this she can do herself, as well as sending for the Elders to have the benefit of their faith" (in *Journal of Discourses,* 13:155). In those times, anointing might have been a way to strengthen the power of faith.

37. *Relief Society Magazine,* January 1965, 5.

38. *Relief Society Magazine,* January 1959, 4. Elder Dallin H. Oaks clarified that President Joseph Fielding Smith's teaching on authority "explains what the Prophet Joseph Smith meant when he said that he organized the Relief Society 'under the priesthood after the pattern of the priesthood.' The authority to be exercised by the officers and teachers of the Relief Society . . . was the authority that would flow to them through their organizational connection with The Church of Jesus Christ of Latter-day Saints and through their individual setting apart under the hands of the priesthood leaders by whom they were called" ("The Relief Society and the Church," *Ensign,* May 1992, 36).

39. Gordon B. Hinckley, "Ten Gifts from the Lord," *Ensign,* November 1985, 87.

40. Dallin H. Oaks, "Two Lines of Communication," *Ensign,* November 2010, 83. In another address, Elder Oaks taught that prayers of faith, whether "uttered alone or in our homes or places of worship, can be effective to heal the sick. Many scriptures refer to the power of faith in the healing of an individual. . . . When the woman who touched Jesus was healed, He told her, 'Thy faith hath made thee whole' (Matthew 9:22)" ("Healing the Sick," *Ensign,* May 2010, 47). Elder Oaks also clarified that "the authority that presides in the family—whether father or

single-parent mother—functions in family matters without the need to get authorization from anyone holding priesthood keys" ("Two Lines of Communication," 86).

41. Boyd K. Packer, "The Relief Society," *Ensign,* May 1998, 73.

42. *Handbook 2, Administering the Church,* 9. Elder Bruce R. McConkie explained the distinction between priesthood keys and priesthood authority: "Every elder . . . has the power to baptize, but no elder can use this power unless he is authorized to do so by someone holding the keys" (*A New Witness for the Articles of Faith* [Salt Lake City: Deseret Book, 1985], 309).

43. Bruce R. McConkie, "The Doctrine of the Priesthood," *Ensign,* May 1982, 32.

44. *Minutes,* April 28, 1842.

45. Verses in the Doctrine and Covenants, including D&C 84:19–22, 33–40; 107:18–20; 121:26–29, 33, are excellent places to begin a study of the fruits and blessings of the Melchizedek Priesthood.

46. Bruce R. McConkie, "Our Sisters from the Beginning," *Ensign,* January 1979, 61.

47. D&C 131:2.

48. D&C 132: 16, 19.

49. John A. Widtsoe, *Priesthood and Church Government* (Salt Lake City: Deseret Book, 1962), 83; emphasis added.

50. *Minutes,* April 28, 1842.

51. D&C 84:19.

52. D&C 107:18.

53. Said Joseph Smith: "God hath not revealed anything to Joseph, but what He will make known unto the Twelve, and even the least Saint may know all things as fast as he is able to bear them, for the day must come when no man need say to his neighbor, Know ye the Lord; for all shall know Him (who remain) from the least to the greatest" (*Teachings of the Prophet Joseph Smith,* Joseph Fielding Smith, comp. [Salt Lake City: Deseret Book, 1976], 149).

54. D&C 84:33–34.

55. D&C 84:35–40; emphasis added.

56. D&C 25:1.

57. 3 Nephi 9:16–17.

58. *Teachings of the Prophet Joseph Smith,* 166–67.

59. In *Journal of Discourses,* 6:286.

60. *History of the Church,* 4:492.

61. In Journal History, March 4, 1844, Church History Library.

62. *Minutes,* April 28, 1842.

63. *Minutes,* August 13, 1843.

64. The Prophet then explained that "after this instruction, you will be responsible for your

own sins. It is an honor," he said, "to save yourselves—all are responsible to save themselves" (*Minutes*, April 28, 1842).

65. *Minutes,* August 31, 1842.

66. *Minutes,* April 28, 1842.

67. *Minutes,* May 27, 1842.

68. *Minutes,* March 30, 1842. See also *The Words of Joseph Smith,* comp. and ed. by Andrew F. Ehat and Lyndon W. Cook (Salt Lake City: Bookcraft, 1980), 137 fn4.

69. James E. Talmage, "The Eternity of Sex," *Young Woman's Journal,* October 1914, 25:602–3.

70. *History of the Church,* 4:604.

71. Joseph Smith instructed those men "in the principles and order of the Priesthood, attending to washings, anointings, endowments and the communication of keys pertaining to the Aaronic Priesthood, and so on to the highest order of the Melchisedek Priesthood. . . . In this council was instituted the ancient order of things for the first time in these last days" (*History of the Church,* 5:1–2). The seven men were: Hyrum Smith, Brigham Young, Heber C. Kimball, Newel K. Whitney, Willard Richards, George Miller, and James Adams.

72. *History of the Church,* 5:2.

73. Joseph Smith, quoted by Mercy Fielding Thompson, in "Recollections of the Prophet Joseph Smith," *Juvenile Instructor,* July 1, 1892, 400.

74. Elizabeth Ann Whitney, "A Leaf from an Autobiography," *Woman's Exponent,* February 15, 1879, 191.

75. *History of the Church,* 7:567.

76. Sarah DeArmon Pea Rich, "Autobiography 1885–93," Church History Library, 66. See also Richard G. Scott, "Temple Worship: The Source of Strength and Power in Times of Need," *Ensign,* May 2009, 44–45.

77. Howard W. Hunter, "Exceeding Great and Precious Promises," *Ensign,* November 1994, 8.

78. See Tad R. Callister, *The Infinite Atonement* (Salt Lake City: Deseret Book, 2000), 293. Said Brigham Young: "Let me give you a definition in brief. Your endowment is, to receive all those ordinances in the house of the Lord, which are necessary for you, after you have departed this life, to enable you to walk back to the presence of the Father, passing the angels who stand as sentinels, . . . and gain your eternal exaltation" (*Discourses of Brigham Young* [Salt Lake City: Deseret Book, 1975], 416).

79. Thomas S. Monson, "The Holy Temple—A Beacon to the World," *Ensign,* May 2011, 93; emphasis added.

80. Douglas L. Callister, address at Davis County Young Single Adult Fireside, April 17, 2011.

81. John A. Widtsoe, "Temple Worship," *Utah Genealogical and Historical Magazine,* April 1921, 63.

82. *History of the Church,* 3:295.

83. D&C 95:8.

84. D&C 109:13, 15, 22, 38.

85. See D&C 121:45.

86. *Minutes,* April 28, 1842.

87. See D&C 76:66–67; 107:19.

88. *Minutes,* June 9, 1842.

89. *Minutes,* June 9, 1842. President Joseph F. Smith elaborated on the purpose of Relief Society when he stated that the sisters were to "look after the spiritual welfare and salvation of the mothers and daughters of Zion; to see that none is neglected, but that all are guarded against misfortune, calamity, the powers of darkness, and the evils that threaten them in the world." (*Gospel Doctrine* [Salt Lake City: Deseret Book, 1999], 385.)

90. *Minutes,* April 28, 1842.

91. *Minutes,* March 17, 1842.

92. *Minutes,* March 30, 1842.

93. *Minutes,* April 28, 1842.

94. *Minutes,* May 26, 1842.

95. *Minutes,* June 9, 1842.

96. *Minutes,* August 31, 1842.

97. *Minutes,* June 9, 1842.

98. Helen Mar Whitney, "Scenes and Incidents at Winter Quarters," *Woman's Exponent,* December 1, 1885, 98.

99. 2 Timothy 3:6–7.

100. 2 Nephi 13:16.

101. *Minutes,* April 28, 1842.

102. Moroni 7:48.

103. Mosiah 28:3.

104. *Minutes,* June 9, 1842.

105. *Teachings of Gordon B. Hinckley* (Salt Lake City: Deseret Book, 1997), 597.

106. Thomas S. Monson, "What Have I Done for Someone Today?" *Ensign,* November 2009, 85.

107. Henry B. Eyring, "Our Hearts Knit as One," *Ensign,* November 2008, 68.

108. Gordon B. Hinckley, "Daughters of God," *Ensign,* November 1991, 99.

109. In *Journal of Discourses,* 10:167.

110. 2 Nephi 32:7.

111. Boyd K. Packer, "The Relief Society," *Ensign,* November 1978, 9.

To the Female Relief Society of Nauvoo

March 17, March 30, April 28,

May 26, June 9, August 31, 1842

MARCH 17, 1842

✦✿✦

Prest. Smith, & Elders Taylor & Richards return'd and the meeting was address'd by Prest. Smith, to illustrate the object of the Society—that the Society of Sisters might provoke the brethren to good works in looking to the wants of the poor—searching after objects of charity, and in administering to their wants—to assist; by correcting the morals and strengthening the virtues of the female community, and save the Elders the trouble of rebuking; that they may give their time to other duties &c. in their public teaching.

Prest. Smith further remark'd that an organization to show them how to go to work would be sufficient. He propos'd that the Sisters elect a presiding officer to preside over them, and let that presiding officer choose two

Counsellors to assist in the duties of her Office—that he would ordain them to preside over the Society—and let them preside just as the Presidency, preside over the church; and if they need his instruction—ask him, he will give it from time to time.

Let this Presidency serve as a constitution—all their decisions be considered law; and acted upon as such.

If any Officers are wanted to carry out the designs of the Institution, let them be appointed and set apart, as Deacons, Teachers &c. are among us.

The minutes of your meetings will be precedents for you to act upon—your Constitution and law.

He then suggested the propriety of electing a Presidency to continue in office during good behavior, or so long as they shall continue to fill the office with dignity &c. like the first Presidency of the church.

Motioned by Sister Whitney and seconded by Sister Packard that Mrs. Emma Smith be chosen President—passed unanimously—

Mov'd by Prest. Smith, that Mrs. Smith proceed to

NOTES

choose her Counsellors, that they may be ordain'd to preside over this Society, in taking care of the poor—administering to their wants, and attending to the various affairs of this Institution.

The Presidentess Elect, then made choice of Mrs. Sarah M. Cleveland and Mrs. Elizabeth Ann Whitney for Counsellors—

President Smith read the Revelation to Emma Smith, from the book of Doctrine and Covenants; and stated that she was ordain'd at the time, the Revelation was given, to expound the scriptures to all; and to teach the female part of community; and that not she alone, but others, may attain to the same blessings.—

The 2d Epistle of John, 1st verse, was then read to show that respect was then had to the same thing; and that why she was called an Elect lady is because, elected to preside....

Prest. Smith then resumed his remarks and gave instruction how to govern themselves in their

NOTES

91

meetings—when one wishes to speak, address the chair—and the chairman responds to the address.

Should two speak at once, the Chair shall decide who speaks first, if any one is dissatisfied, she appeals to the house—

When one has the floor, occupies as long as she pleases.

Proper manner of address is Mrs. Chairman or President and not Mr. Chairman &c.

A question can never be put until it has a second

When the subject for discussion has been fairly investigated; the Chairman will say, are you ready for the question? &c.

Whatever the majority of the house decide upon becomes a law to the Society.

Prest. Smith proceeded to give counsel;—Do not injure the character of any one—if members of the Society shall conduct improperly, deal with them, and keep all your doings within your own bosoms, and hold all characters sacred—....

NOTES

Prest. Smith continued instructions to the Chair to suggest to the members anything the chair might wish, and which it might not be proper for the chair to put, or move &c.

Mov'd by Counsellor Cleveland, and secon'd by Counsellor Whitney, that this Society be called <u>The Nauvoo Female Relief</u> Society.

Elder Taylor offered an amendment, that it be called <u>The Nauvoo Female Benevolent Society</u> which would give a more definite and extended idea of the Institution—that Relief be struck out and Benevolent inserted.

Prest. Smith offer'd instruction on votes—

The motion was seconded by Counsellor Cleveland and unanimously carried, on the amendment by Elder Taylor.

The Prest. then suggested that she would like an argument with Elder Taylor on the words Relief and Benevolence.

NOTES

Prest. J. Smith mov'd that the vote for amendment, be rescinded, which was carried—

Motion for adjournment by Elder Richards and objected by Prest. J. Smith.—

Prest. J. Smith—Benevolent is a popular term—and the term <u>Relief</u> is not known among popular Societies—<u>Relief</u> is more extended in its signification than <u>Benevolent</u> and might extend to the liberation of the culprit—and might be wrongly construed by our enemies to say that the Society was to relieve criminals from punishment &c. &c—to relieve a murderer, which would not be a benevolent act—

Prest. Emma Smith, said the <u>popularity</u> of the word benevolent is one great objection—no person can think of the word as associated with public Institutions, without thinking of the Washingtonian Benevolent Society which was one of the most corrupt Institutions of the day—do not wish to have it call'd after other Societies in the world—

Prest. J. Smith arose to state that he had no objection

NOTES

_____

_____

_____

_____

to the word <u>Relief</u>—that on question they ought to deliberate candidly and investigate all subjects.

Counsellor Cleveland arose to remark concerning the question before the house, that we should not regard the idle speech of our enemies—we design to act in the name of the Lord—to relieve the wants of the distressed, and do all the good we can.—

Eliza R. Snow arose and said that she felt to concur with the President, with regard to the word Benevolent, that many Societies with which it had been associated, were corrupt,—that the popular Institutions of the day should not be our guide—that as daughters of Zion, we should set an example for all the world, rather than confine ourselves to the course which had been heretofore pursued—one objection to the word <u>Relief</u> is that the idea associated with it is that of some great calamity—that we intend appropriating on some extraordinary occasions instead of meeting the common occurrences—

Prest. Emma Smith remark'd—we are going to do something <u>extraordinary</u>—when a boat is stuck on the

NOTES

rapids with a multitude of Mormons on board we shall consider <u>that</u> a loud call for <u>relief</u>—we expect extraordinary occasions and pressing calls—

Elder Taylor arose and said—I shall have to concede the point—your arguments are so potent I cannot stand before them—I shall have to give way—

Prest. J. S. said I also shall have to concede the point, all I shall have to give to the poor, I shall give to this Society—

Counsellor Whitney mov'd, that this Society be call'd <u>The Nauvoo Female Relief Society</u>—secon'd by Counsellor Cleveland—

E. R. Snow offer'd an amendment by way of transposition of words, instead of The <u>Nauvoo Female Relief Society,</u> it shall be call'd The <u>Female Relief Society</u> of Nauvoo—Seconded by Prest. J. Smith and carried—

The previous question was then put—Shall this Society be call'd <u>The Female Relief Society</u> of <u>Nauvoo?</u>—carried unanimously.—

Prest. J. Smith—I now declare this Society organiz'd

NOTES

with President and Counsellors &c. according to Parliamentary usages—and all who shall hereafter be admitted into this Society must be free from censure and receiv'd by vote—

Prest. J. Smith offered—$5.00 in gold piece to commence the funds of the Institution.

Prest. Emma Smith requested that the gentlemen withdraw before they proceed to the choice of Secretary and Treasurer, as was mov'd by Prest. J. Smith—

NOTES

MARCH 30, 1842

❧ ✿ ☙

Prest. J. Smith arose—spoke of the organization of the Society—said he was deeply interested that it might be built up to the Most High in an acceptable manner—that its rules must be observed—that none should be received into the Society but those who were worthy—propos'd that the Society go into a close examination of every candidate—that they were going too fast—that the Society should grow up by degrees—should commence with a few individuals—thus have a select Society of the virtuous and those who will walk circumspectly—commended them for their zeal but said sometimes their zeal was not according to knowledge—One principal object of the Institution was to purge out iniquity—said they must be extremely careful in all their examinations or the consequences would be serious

Said all difficulties which might & would cross our way must be surmounted, though the soul be <u>tried,</u> the heart faint, and hands hang down—must not retrace our steps—that there must be decision of character aside from sympathy—that when instructed we must obey that voice, observe the Constitution that the blessings of heaven may rest down upon us—all must act in concert or nothing can be done—that the Society should move according to the ancient Priesthood, hence there should be a select Society separate from all the evils of the world, choice, virtuous and holy—Said he was going to make of this Society a kingdom of priests as in Enoch's day—as in Pauls day—that it is the privilege of each member to live long and enjoy health—Prest Smith propos'd that the ladies [gentlemen] withdraw, that the Society might proceed to business—that those wishing to join should have their names presented at the next meeting—

Prest. J. Smith withdrew—

NOTES

APRIL 28, 1842

🌿❀🌿

President Smith arose and said that the purport of his being present on the occasion was, to make observations respecting the Priesthood, and give instructions for the benefit of the Society That as his instructions were intended only for the Society; he requested that a vote should be taken on those present who were not members, to ascertain whether they should be admitted—he exhorted the meeting to act honestly and uprightly in all their proceedings inasmuch as they would be call'd to give an account to Jehovah. All hearts must repent—be pure and God will regard them and bless them in a manner that they could not be bless'd in any other way—....
[Votes were then taken on the women to be included.]

Prest. J. Smith arose and call'd the attention of the

meeting to the 12th Chap. of 1st Cor. "Now concerning spiritual gifts" &c.—Said that the passage which reads "no man can <u>say</u> that Jesus is the the Lord but by the holy ghost," should be translated, no man can <u>know</u> &c

He continued to read the Chap. and give instructions respecting the different offices, and the necessity of every individual acting in the sphere allotted him or her; and filling the several offices to which they were appointed—Spoke of the disposition of man, to consider the lower offices in the church dishonorable and to look with jealous eyes upon the standing of others—that it was the nonsense of the human heart, for a person to be aspiring to other stations than appointed of God—that it was better for individuals to magnify their respective callings, and wait patiently till God shall say to them come up higher. He said the reason of these remarks being made, was, that some little thing was circulating in the Society, that some persons were not going right in laying hands on the sick &c. Said if he had common sympathies, would rejoice that the sick could be heal'd,

NOTES

that the time had not been before, that these things could be in their proper order—that the church is not now organiz'd in its proper order, and cannot be until the Temple is completed—Prest. Smith continued the subject by adverting to the commission given to the ancient apostles "Go ye into all the world" &c.—no matter who believeth; these signs, such as healing the sick, casting out devils &c. should follow all that believe whether male or female. He ask'd this Society if they could not see by this sweeping stroke, that wherein they are ordained, it is the privilege of those set apart to administer in that authority which is confer'd on them—and if the sisters should have faith to heal the sick, let all hold their tongues, and let every thing roll on.

He said, if God has appointed him, and chosen him as an instrument to lead the church, why not let him lead it through? Why stand in the way, when he is appointed to do a thing? Who knows the mind of God? Does he not reveal things differently from what we expect? He remark'd that he was continually rising—altho' he

NOTES

_____

_____

_____

_____

had every thing bearing him down, standing in his way and opposing—after all he always comes out right in the end.

Respecting the female laying on hands, he further remark'd, there could be no devils in it if God gave his sanction by healing—that there could be no more sin in any female laying hands on the sick than in wetting the face with water—that it is no sin for any body to do it that has faith, or if the sick has faith to be heal'd by the administration.

He reprov'd those that were dispos'd to find fault with the management of concerns—saying if he undertook to lead the church he would lead it right—that he calculates to organize the church in proper order &c.

President Smith continued by speaking of the difficulties he had to surmount ever since the commencement of the work in consequence of aspiring men, "great big Elders" as he called them, who had caused him much trouble, whom he had taught in the private counsel; and they would go forth into the world and p[r]oclaim the

NOTES

things he had taught them; as their own revelations—
said the same aspiring disposition will be in this Society,
and must be guarded against—that every person should
stand and act in the place appointed, and thus sanctify
the Society and get it pure—

He said he had been trampled underfoot by aspiring Elders, for all were infected with that spirit, for in-
stance P. Pratt[,] O. Pratt, O. Hyde and J. Page had been
aspiring—they could not be exalted but must run away
as tho' the care and authority of the church were vested
with them—he said we had a subtle devil to deal with,
and could only curb him by being humble.

He said as he had this opportunity, he was going
to instruct the Society and point out the way for them
to conduct, that they might act according to the will of
God—that he did not know as he should have many opportunities of teaching them—that they were going to
be left to themselves,—they would not long have him
to instruct them—that the church would not have his
instruction long, and the world would not be troubled

NOTES

with him a great while, and would not have his teachings—He spoke of delivering the keys to this Society and to the church—that according to his prayers God had appointed him elsewhere

He exhorted the sisters always to concentrate their faith and prayers for, and place confidence in those whom God has appointed to honor, whom God has plac'd at the head to lead—that we should arm them with our prayers.—that the keys of the kingdom are about to be given to them, that they may be able to detect every thing false—as well as to the Elders

He said if one member becomes corrupt and you know it; you must immediately put it away. The sympathies of the heads of the church have induc'd them to bear with those that were corrupt; in consequence of which all become contaminated—you must put down iniquity and by your good example provoke the Elders to good works—if you do right, no danger of going too fast: he said he did not care how fast we run in the path of virtue. Resist evil and there is no danger. God, men,

NOTES

angels, and devils can't condemn those that resist every thing that is evil—as well might the devil seek to dethrone Jehovah, as that soul that resists every thing that is evil.

The charitable Society—this is according to your natures—it is natural for females to have feelings of charity—you are now plac'd in a situation where you can act according to those sympathies which God has planted in your bosoms. If you live up to these principles how great and glorious!—if you live up to your privileges, the angels cannot be restrain'd from being your associates—females, if they are pure and innocent can come into the presence of God; for what is more pleasing to God than innocence; you must be innocent or you cannot come up before God. If we would come before God let us be pure ourselves. The devil has great power—he will so transform things as to make one gape at those who are doing the will of God—You need not be tearing men for their deeds, but let the weight of innocence be felt; which is more mighty than a millstone hung about

NOTES

the neck. Not war, not jangle, not contradiction, but meekness, love, purity, these are the things that should magnify us.—Achan must be brought to light—iniquity must be purged out—<u>then</u> the vail will be rent and the blessings of heaven will flow down—they will roll down like the Missisippi river. This Society shall have power to command Queens in their midst—I now deliver it as a prophecy that before ten years shall roll round, the queens of the earth shall come and pay their respects to this Society—they shall come with their millions and shall contribute of their abundance for the relief of the poor—If you will be pure, nothing can hinder.

After this instruction, you will be responsible for your own sins. It is an honor to save yourselves—all are responsible to save themselves.

Prest. Smith, after reading from the above mentioned Chapter, continued to give instruction respecting the order of God, as established in the church; saying every one should aspire only to magnify his own office &c.—

NOTES

He then commenc'd reading the 13th chapter, "Though I speak with the tongues of men" &c; and said don't be limited in your views with regard to your neighbors' virtues, but be limited towards your own virtues, and not think yourselves more righteous than others; you must enlarge your souls toward others if yould [you would?] do like Jesus, and carry your fellow creatures to Abram's bosom.

He said he had manifested long suffering and we must do so too—Prest. Smith then read, "Though I have the gift of prophecy" &c. He then said, though one should become mighty—do great things—overturn mountains &c and should then turn to eat and drink with the drunken; all former deeds would not save him—but he would go to destruction!

As you increase in innocence and virtue, as you increase in goodness, let your hearts expand—let them be enlarged towards others—you must be longsuff'ring and bear with the faults and errors of mankind. How precious are the souls of men!—The female part of

NOTES

community are apt to be contracted in their views. You must not be contracted, but you must be liberal in your feelings.

Let this Society teach how to act towards husbands to treat them with mildness and affection. When a man is borne down with trouble—when he is perplex'd, if he can meet a smile, an argument—if he can meet with mildness, it will calm down his soul and soothe his feelings. When the mind is going to despair, it needs a solace.

This Society is to get instruction thro' the order which God has established—thro' the medium of those appointed to lead—and I now turn the key to you in the name of God and this Society shall rejoice and knowledge and intelligence shall flow down from this time—this is the beginning of better days, to this Society

When you go home never give a cross word, but let kindness, charity and love, crown your works henceforward. Don't envy sinners—have mercy on them. God will destroy them.—Let your labors be confin'd mostly

NOTES

_____

_____

_____

_____

to those around you in your own circle; as far as knowledge is concerned, it may extend to all the world, but your administrations, should be confin'd to the circle of your immediate acquaintance, and more especially to the members of the Society.

Those ordain'd to lead the Society, are authoriz'd to appoint to different offices as the circumstances shall require.

If any have a matter to reveal, let it be in your own tongue. Do not indulge too much in the gift of tongues, or the devil will take advantage of the innocent. You may speak in tongues for your comfort but I lay this down for a rule that if any thing is taught by the gift of tongues, it is not to be received for doctrine.

Prest. S. then offered instruction respecting the propriety of females administering to the sick by the laying on of hands—said it was according to revelation &c. said he never was plac'd in similar circumstances, and never had given the same instruction.

NOTES

He clos'd his instructions by expressing his satisfaction in improving the opportunity.

The spirit of the Lord was pour'd out in a very powerful manner, never to be forgotten by those present on that interesting occasion.

NOTES

MAY 26, 1842

❧❀☙

Prest. J. Smith rose, read the 14th Chap. of Ezekiel—said the Lord had declar'd by the prophet that the people should each one stand for himself and depend on no man or men in that state of corruption of the Jewish church—that righteous persons could only deliver their own souls—app[l]ied it to the present state of the church of Latter-Day Saints—said if the people departed from the Lord, they must fall—that they were depending on the prophet hence were darkened in their minds from neglect of themselves—envious toward the innocent, while they afflict the virtuous with their shafts of envy.

There is another error which opens a door for the adversary to enter. As females possess refin'd feelings and sensitivenes[s], they are also subject to an overmuch zeal which must ever prove dangerous, and cause them to be rigid in a religious capacity—should be arm'd with mercy notwithstanding the iniquity among us. Said he had been instrumental in bringing it to light—melancholy and awful that so many are under the condemnation of the devil & going to perdition.

With deep feeling said that they are our fellows—we lov'd them once. Shall we not encourage them to reformation?

We have not forgiven them seventy times—perhaps we have not forgiven them once. There is now a day of salvation to such as repent and reform—they should be cast out from this Society, yet we should woo them to return to God lest they escape not the damnation of hell!

When there is a mountain top there also is a vally—we should act in all things as a proper medium—to every immortal spirit. Notwithstanding the unworthy are among us, the virtuous should not from self-importance grieve and oppress needlessly those unfortunate ones, even these should be encourag'd to hereafter live to be

NOTES

honored by this Society who are the best portions of community. Said he had two things to recommend to the Society, to put a double watch over the tongue. No organiz'd body can exist without this at all. All organiz'd bodies have their peculiar evils, weaknesses and difficulties—the object is to make those not so good, equal with the good and ever hold the keys of pow'r which will influence to virtue and goodness. Should chasten and reprove and keep it all in silence, not even mention them again, then you will be established in power, virtue and holiness and the wrath of God will be turn'd away. One request to the Prest. and Society, that you search yourselves—the tongue is an unruly member—hold your tongues about things of no moment,—a little tale will set the world on fire. At this time the truth on the guilty should not be told openly—Strange as this may seem, yet this is policy. We must use precaution in bringing sinners to justice lest in exposing these heinous sins, we draw the indignation of a gentile world upon us (and to their imagination justly too)

NOTES

It is necessary to hold an influence in the world and thus spare ourselves an extermination; and also accomplish our end in spreading the gospel or holiness in the earth.

If we were brought to desolation, the disobedient would find no help. There are some who are obedient yet men cannot steady the ark—my arm can not do it—God must steady it. To the iniquitous show yourselves merciful. I am advis'd by some of the heads of the church to tell the Relief Society to be virtuous—but to save the church from desolation and the sword beware, be still, be prudent. Repent, reform but do it in a way to not destroy all around you. I do not want to cloak iniquity—all things contrary to the will of God, should be cast from us, but dont do more hurt than good with your tongues—be pure in heart—Jesus designs to save the people out of their sins. Said Jesus ye shall do the work which ye see me do. These are the grand key words for the Society to act upon.

If I were not in your midst to aid and council you,

NOTES

the devil would overcome you. I want the innocent to go free—rather spare ten iniquitous among you than than condemn one innocent one. "Fret not thyself because of evil doers." God will see to it.

NOTES

JUNE 9, 1842

❧ ♣ ☙

Prest J. Smith opened the meeting by pray'r and proceeded to address the congregation on the design of the Institution—said it is no matter how fast the Society increases if all are virtuous—that we must be as particular with regard to the character of members as when the Society first started—that sometimes persons wish to put themselves into a Society of this kind, when they do not intend to pursue the ways of purity and righteousness, as if the Society would be a shelter to them in their iniquity.

Prest. S. said that henceforth no person shall be admitted but by presenting regular petitions signed by two or three members in good standing in the Society—whoever comes in must be of good report.

Harriet Luce and Mary Luce were receiv'd into the Society by recommend.

Objections previously made against Mahala Overton were remov'd—after which Prest Smith continued his address—said he was going to preach mercy Supposing that Jesus Christ and angels should object to us on frivolous things, what would become of us? We must be merciful and overlook small things.

Respecting the reception of Sis. Overton, Prest. Smith [said] It grieves me that there is no fuller fellowship—if one member suffer all feel it—by union of feeling we obtain pow'r with God. Christ said he came to call sinners to repentance and save them. Christ was condemn'd by the righteous jews because he took sinners into his society—he took them upon the principle that they repented of their sins. It is the object of this Society to reform persons, not to take those that are corrupt, but if they repent we are bound to take them and by kindness sanctify and cleanse from all unrighteousness, by our influence in watching over them—nothing will have such

NOTES

influence over people, as the fear of being disfellowship'd by so goodly a Society as this. Then take Sis. O. as Jesus received sinners into his bosom. . . .

Nothing is so much calculated to lead people to forsake sin as to take them by the hand and watch over them with tenderness. When persons manifest the least kindness and love to me, O what pow'r it has over my mind, while the opposite course has a tendency to harrow up all the harsh feelings and depress the human mind.

It is one evidence that men are unacquainted with the principle of godliness, to behold the contraction of feeling and lack of charity. The pow'r and glory of Godliness is spread out on a broad principle to throw out the mantle of charity. God does not look on sin with allowance, but when men have sin'd there must be allowance made for them.

All the religious world is boasting of righteousness—tis the doctrine of the devil to retard the human mind and retard our progress, by filling us with selfrighteousness—The nearer we get to our heavenly Father, the

NOTES

more are we dispos'd to look with compassion on perishing souls—to take them upon our shoulders and cast
their sins behind our back. I am going to talk to all this
Society—if you would have God have mercy on you,
have mercy on one another.

Prest. S. then refer'd them to the conduct of the
Savior when he was taken and crucified &c.

He then made a promise in the name of the Lord
saying, that soul that has righteousness enough to ask
God in the secret place for life, every day of their lives
shall live to three score years & ten—We must walk uprightly all day long—How glorious are the principles of
righteousness! We are full of selfishness—the devil flatters us that we are very righteous, while we are feeding
on the faults of others—We can only live by worshipping
our God—all must do it for themselves—none can do it
for another. How mild the Savior dealt with Peter, saying
"when thou art converted, strengthen thy brethren"—
at an other time he said to him "lovest thou me? 'Feed
my sheep.'"—If the sisters love the Lord let them feed the

NOTES

_____

_____

_____

_____

sheep and not destroy them. How oft have wise men & women sought to dictate br. Joseph by saying "O if I were br. Joseph I would do this and that." But if they were in br. Joseph's shoes, they would find that men could not be compel'd into the kingdom of God, but must be dealt with in long suff'ring—and at last we shall save them. The way to keep all the saints together and keep the work rolling, is to wait with all long suff'ring till God shall bring such characters to justice. There should be no license for sin, but mercy should go hand in hand with reproof.

Sisters of this Society, shall there be strife among you? I will not have it—you must repent and get the love of God. Away with selfrighteousness. The best measure or principle to bring the poor to repentance is to administer to their wants—the Society is not only to relieve the poor, but to save souls.

Prest. S. then said that he would give a lot of land to the Society by deeding it to the Treasurer, that the Society may build houses for the poor. He also said he

NOTES

would give a house—frame not finished—said that br. Cahoon will move it on to the aforesaid lot, and the Society can pay him by giving Orders on the Store—that it was a good plan to set those to work who are owing widows and thus make an offsett &c. &c.

NOTES

AUGUST 31, 1842

❧❀❦

Prest. Joseph Smith opened the meeting by addressing the Society. He commenced by expressing his happiness and thankfulness for the privilege of being present on the occasion. He said that great exertions had been made on the part of our enemies, but they had not accomplished their purpose. God had enabled him to keep out of their hands—he had war'd a good warfare inasmuch as he had whip'd out all of Bennett's host—his feelings at the present time were, that inasmuch as the Lord Almighty had preserv'd him today. He said it reminded him of the Savior, when he said to the pharisees, "Go ye and tell that fox, Behold I cast out devils, and I do cures today and tomorrow, and the third day I shall be perfected." &c.

He said he expected the heavenly Father had decreed that the Missourians shall not get him—if they do, it will be because he does not keep out of the way.

Prest. S. continued by saying, I shall triumph over my enemies—I have begun to triumph over them at home and I shall do it abroad—all those that rise up against me will feel the weight of their iniquity upon their own heads—those that speak evil are abominable characters—and full of iniquity—All the fuss and all the stir against me, is like the jack in the lantern, it cannot be found. Altho' I do wrong, I do not the wrongs that I am charg'd with doing—the wrong that I do is thro' the frailty of human nature like other men. No man lives without fault. Do you think that even Jesus, if he were here would be without fault in your eyes? They said all manner of evil against him—they all watch'd for iniquity.

How easy it was for Jesus to call out all the iniquity of the hearts of those whom he was among? The servants of the Lord are required to guard against those

NOTES

_____

_____

_____

_____

things that are calculated to do the most evil—the little foxes spoil the vines—little evils do the most injury to the church. If you have evil feelings and speak of them to one another, it has a tendency to do mischief—these things result in those evils which are calculated to cut the throats of the heads of the church.

When I do the best I can—when I am accomplishing the greatest good, then the most evils are got up against me. I would to God that you would be wise.

I now counsel you, if you know anything, hold your tongues, and the least harm will be done.

The Female Relief Society has taken the most active part in my welfare—against my enemies—in petitioning to the Governor—These measures were all necessary— Do you not see that I foresaw what was coming before-hand, by the spirit of prophesy?—All had an influence in my redemption from the hand of my enemies.

If these measures had not been taken, more serious consequences would have resulted.

I have come here to bless you. The Society has

NOTES

done well—their principles are to practice holiness. God loves you and your prayers in my behalf shall avail much—Let them not cease to ascend to God in my behalf. The enemy will never get weary—I expect he will array every thing against me—I expect tremendous warfare. He that will war the Christian warfare will have the angels of devils and all the infernal powers of darkness continually array'd against him. When wicked and corrupt men oppose, it is a criterion to judge if a man is warring the christian warfare. When all men speak evil of you, blessed are ye &c. Shall a man be considered bad, when men speak evil of him? No: If a man stands and opposes the world of sin, he may expect all things array'd against him.

But it will be but a little season and all these afflictions will be turn'd away from us inasmuch as we are faithful and are not overcome by these evils. By seeing the blessings of the endowment rolling on, and the kingdom increasing and spreading from sea to sea; we will rejoice that we were not overcome by these foolish things.

NOTES

Prest. S. then remark'd that a few things had been manifested to him in his absence, respecting the baptisms for the dead, which he should communicate next sabbath if nothing should occur to prevent.

Prest. S. then address'd the throne of Grace.

NOTES

_____

_____

_____

_____

INDEX

❧✿❧

INDEX

INDEX